THE UNITED STATES OF AMERICA

UNITED NATIONS RESEARCH INSTITUTE
FOR SOCIAL DEVELOPMENT - GENEVA

Publications Series: Regional Planning

Antoni Kuklinski
Editor

Volume 2

MOUTON · PARIS · THE HAGUE

Regional Development Experiences and Prospects in the United States of America

John H. Cumberland
Professor of Economics, University of Maryland

MOUTON · PARIS · THE HAGUE

The United Nations Research Institute for Social Development is an autonomous United Nations activity, established for the purpose of conducting research into 'problems and policies of social development and relationships between various types of social development and economic development during different phases of economic growth'. The publications of the Institute are intended to contribute to
(a) the work of the United Nations Secretariat in the field of social policy, social development planning and balanced economic and social development;
(b) regional planning institutes set up under the auspices of the United Nations;
(c) national institutes in the field of economic and/or social development and planning.
Although UNRISD takes general responsibility for this publication, the opinions expressed by the authors do not necessarily reflect the views of the Institute.

Regional Planning

1. Regional Development: Experiences and Prospects in South and Southeast Asia
2. Regional Development: Experiences and Prospects in the United States of America
3. Regional Development: Experiences and Prospects in Latin America
4. Regional Development: Experiences and Prospects in Eastern Europe
5. Growth Poles and Growth Centres in Regional Planning
6. Regional Information and Regional Planning
7. Regional Sociology, Environment and Regional Planning
8. Regional Disaggregation of National Policies and Plans
9. Growth Poles and Growth Centres as Instruments of Modernization in Developing Countries
10. Urban-regional Development in South America: A Process of Diffusion and Integration

Library of Congress Catalog Card Number: 73-163629

Jacket design by Françoise Rojare

 Second edition, 1973

Printed in the Netherlands

To Agnes and Laurence L. Cumberland

Preface by the Director of UNRISD

This is the second volume in an international series of studies on experiences and prospects of regional development undertaken by the United Nations Research Institute for Social Development. The series has been organized and edited at the Institute by Dr. Antoni R. Kuklinski.

The present study on regional development in the United States by John Cumberland has been made possible by an arrangement with Resources for the Future, Inc. The Institute is grateful for this generous contribution by Resources for the Future and is happy to have Professor Cumberland's study for the series.

The United States has had a rich and varied experience in regional development and planning. It offers a unique laboratory for research on regional problems because of its size, its geographical differentiations and the relative development of regional statistics and records. Professor Cumberland has approached the subject with enthusiasm and with a fresh look at some old problems.

Donald V. McGranahan
Director

Preface by the Director of the Regional and Urban Studies Program of Resources for the Future, Inc.

The growth of interest in the problems of stagnant regions in developing countries during the 1960's was accompanied by an awareness of the practical shortcomings of the fund of knowledge and information available to regional planners and national policy makers around the world for coping with lagging regions in developing countries. It was not as though no experience had been accumulated to draw upon – indeed, major regional development projects had been launched in various parts of the world in the two decades following World War II. Several of these were well advanced: the SUDENE program in Northeast Brazil, the Mezzogiorno project in Southern Italy, the programs for the development of the Guayana region in Venezuela, the Gomilla project in Pakistan, the Aswan regional development program on the Nile and numerous smaller projects. More projects were being drawn up, posing the danger that each would have to 're-invent the wheel' – to make the same mistakes made earlier, to learn out of a costly trial and error process what kinds of policies worked and which ones yielded little.

In 1965 the United Nations launched its Regional Development program as an effort to accelerate and institutionalize the social learning processes concerning regional development. The research component of the Program was allocated to UNRISD, which started its activities in this field in 1967. The basic concept around which this program was organized was to reap the lessons of earlier and current regional development experiences in the hope of accumulating some general propositions about the planning and practice of regional development which had wide applicability in time and place. The basic instrument was to be the carefully documented case study of individual efforts.

In anticipation of such an effort, the virtues of having a broad look at the themes and styles of regional development efforts around the world become obvious, especially since the world is easily sectored into several large regions each of whose cultural origins, political institutions, economic organizations and development levels gave it a special kind of policy uniqueness when seen against the others. One such major world region is non-Latin North America.

Resources for the Future, as a private, non-profit research foundation concerned with the role of natural resources and the physical environment in development, had played a consultative role in the birth and development of the United Nations program. Indeed, Harvey Perloff, then an RFF program director, contributed substantially to the U.N. deliberations on strategy and content of the U.N. regional development effort. It was only natural, then, for the Regional Development program under Dr. Antoni R. Kuklinski to turn to RFF for advice on the conduct of the study of regional development in North America. To show its support and continuing interest in the U.N. effort, RFF agreed to assume responsibility for the North American study.

RFF and the U.N. were very fortunate in finding John H. Cumberland of the University of Maryland to be interested and available to carry out this review. Dr. Cumberland's work in regional economics is widely known in the United States and abroad. However, what was especially appealing to RFF and the U.N. was his interest in re-examining the main dimensions of U.S. economic history in the light of implicit national strategies for regional development. These implicit strategies paved the way for the explicit national concern of the U.S. federal government about lagging and chronically depressed regions in an affluent and prosperous economy. These concerns have become embodied in the Appalachian Regional Development Program and the activities of the U.S. Economic Development Administration.

A common reaction of knowledgeable people to this search for lessons from the North American regional development experience to aid developing countries can be expressed in the question 'What experience – beyond the TVA, that is?' Certainly the TVA has become a worldwide symbol of a particular kind of regional development experience. It has become a well-documented text book case in the regional planning curriculum. But is there really nothing left when TVA is disposed of? Cumberland has gone a long way to make the case that successes and failures of almost two hundred years of U.S. internal development policies are rich in lessons – some negative, all germane – for developing nations considering the development of *their* frontiers, the uplifting of the welfare of *their* lagging areas, the use of broad infrastructure policies to reallocate interregionally the major elements of *their* national economies. In so doing, he has not only far exceeded his charge in this review, but provided a new perspective on the history of U.S. economic development that richly complements the extant literature in the field.

The Canadian experience in regional development has been splendidly described in earlier writing by Thomas N. Brewis, who agreed generously, nevertheless, to recap and evaluate it for this project. Because the style and content of the Brewis study are strongly influenced by current, as opposed to historical, public policy, the publishers and sponsors of the North American study succumbed to the logic of letting each stand on its own feet. Hence, the *U.S.* experience is the subject of this study. The Canadian appraisal will be treated separately.

All in all, this tripartite relationship among RFF, the U.N. Regional Development Program and Dr. Cumberland has been a rewarding one, not the least for a scholarly contribution offering at the same time a potent message to regional planners and architects of national internal development policies around the world.

Lowdon Wingo
Resources for the Future
Washington, D. C.
March 1971

Acknowledgments

This brief survey of some aspects of regional development experience in the United States has been undertaken as part of a worldwide study by UNRISD of the regional development process.

The material presented falls far short of comprising a comprehensive detailed historical analysis of the total experience in U.S. regional development. Limitations of time and resources led to an arbitrary assignment of priorities to the subjects to be considered. The study does not attempt to cover the general literature on economic development, location theory, or regional planning. From the wealth of material and experience available, an effort was made to focus attention on those problems which seemed to offer the most relevance to students and planners of economic development in other nations.

Clearly, there is no presumption intended that the U.S. experience in regional development offers a model to be emulated by developing nations. On the contrary, one of the basic conclusions of the study is that national policies and programs for regional development tend to reflect the basic value judgments and cultural structure of a society. This study of the U.S. is intended to indicate some of the options open to an advanced industrial nation and to evaluate some of the successes and failures which have been observed.

The reader may detect much explicit as well as implicit criticism of the U.S. approach to regional development. This critical viewpoint has been consciously adopted in an effort to identify some of the possible opportunities for avoiding mistakes of the past and for improving regional development efforts in the future.

The importance of this effort lies in the fact that the real significance of general economic development is how it operates regionally in space to affect human beings in their particular activities, occupations, and lives. Therefore, the underlying purpose of the study is to explore some opportunities in regional development for improving the quality of human life.

The author is indebted to numerous students and associates who have assisted in many ways during the course of the study. The staff at Resources for the Future, Inc., were particularly generous in devoting time, interest and research support to the study. Harvey S. Perloff was instrumental in conceiving the study and the larger international program of research in regional development of which this is a small part. Following Dr. Perloff's move to the University of California at Los Angeles, his successor as Director of Urban and Regional Studies at RFF, Lowdon Wingo, has carried on with continuing encouragement and unfailing patience. Other members of the RFF staff who have generously given of their time and interest include Joseph L. Fisher, President, Michael F. Brewer, Vice President, John E. Herbert, Secretary-Treasurer, Marion Clawson, Pierre R. Crosson, Edgar S. Dunn, Jr., Irving Hoch, John V. Krutilla, and Jose Ramon Lasuen. The continued interest and support of Dr. Antoni R. Kuklinski of the United Nations has been especially helpful.

Colleagues at the University of Maryland who have provided valuable comments include John Quincy Adams III, Dudley Dillard, John W. Dorsey, Curtis C. Harris, Jr., Martin C. McGuire, Charles E. Olson, Mancur Olson, Jr., Jerry J. Shipley, and Neil Singer. Among others who have provided data, information, and comments are Dr. Harvey A. Garn of the Urban Institute, Ralph R. Widner of the Appalachian Regional Commission, Professor Monroe Newman of the Pennsylvania State University, and Mr. James W. Alsip of the U.S. Department of Commerce, Economic Development Administration, Dr. Charles L. Leven of Washington University, Dr. Anthony H. Pascal of the Rand Corporation, Dr. Edgar M. Hoover of the University of Pittsburgh, and Dr. Niles M. Hansen of the University of Texas. Stimulating comments were also received from Mr. Charles S. Ascher. Particular thanks are owed to Professor T. N. Brewis of Carleton University for agreeing to prepare a companion study on the Canadian experience and for the stimulation and assistance resulting from his participation. Despite the valuable advice and assistance received from these and others too numerous to mention, the usual full responsibility for the findings and conclusions is assumed by the author.

The author is indebted to Mr. Bruce N. Stram, Mr. Craig Simmons, and Mr. Thomas E. Marchessault for able assistance in collecting materials and assisting in their evaluation, and to Mrs. Elizabeth Miller for valued assistance and patience in typing. Above all, particular thanks are due to the author's wife, Charlene Cumberland, and son, Laurence Cumberland, for continuing patience and encouragement.

John H. Cumberland

Preface to the second edition

Rapid advances in the theory and practice of regional development make the appearance of this second edition, though it follows the first by only a few years, an appropriate occasion for adding a brief summary of recent developments in the U.S.

Many of the trends emphasized in the earlier edition appear to have been confirmed by events. The tendency of experimental regional programs to proliferate has resulted in the establishment of two new multistate regional commissions, one for the Old West (North and South Dakota, Wyoming, Nebraska and Montana), and one for the Pacific Northwest (Washington, Oregon and Idaho). The administrative review of these regional commissions, and the growing reluctance to continue further support of the Economic Development Administration in its present form, indicate that the U.S. is entering a period of transition in its approach to regional development.

Disparities between the announced humanitarian justification for regional development and the perceived results of actual programs have led to growing disenchantment with traditional approaches.

While there has been no diminution of the time-honored practice of using the limited job-creation and poverty-reduction potentials of typical physical development projects as a convenient rationale for converting public funds and national resources into private benefits for the influential, the growing concern about national priorities suggests that many of the issues emphasized here are now beginning to have an effective impact upon thinking about U.S. regional development. In particular, the continued failure of economic development programs to aid those who are most needy in both rural and urban regions raises serious questions about the wisdom of spending scarce public funds for ambitious physical development programs and for subsidizing the attraction of industry when alternative approaches emphasizing investment in human capital and amelioration of human problems through improved, coordinated programs of education, training, health care, family planning, welfare and counselling could be much more efficient and effective.

Another important development is the accelerating recognition of conflict between traditional concepts of economic growth and emerging concepts of environmental management. The failure of prices in the private sector to reflect the full social cost of exploiting environmental resources and failure of planning in the public sector to provide comprehensive, integrated management of land use, transportation systems, energy policy, technology control and environmental protection have resulted in serious deterioration of the quality of life.

Programs designed ostensibly for water resource improvement, natural resource development, transportation systems, energy supply and other forms of regional development are being increasingly recognized as generating excessively high costs in congestion, noise pollution and a severely degraded quality of life and environment.

As was anticipated from theories of materials balance and environmental economics, many regions are now discovering that ominous environmental problems are arising from the pollutants generated by pollution control processes. Furthermore, the human tendancy to adopt measures which transfer pollution problems elsewhere is raising complex new problems of interregional competition, efficiency and equity. The result has been a fundamental re-evaluation of attitudes toward economic development with growing numbers of regions adopting policies to reduce and in some cases even to halt further growth in population and economic activity rather than suffer the environmental damage associated with current patterns of economic development.

In attempting to chart a balanced course between the compelling rival claims of environment and development, regional planners are necessarily seeking guidelines from numerous disciplines. For example, the environmental impact statement which is now required to accompany all major proposals for federal development programs has turned out to be an unexpectedly potent social invention, which is gradually being adopted at the state and local levels. While few experts (even among economists) would rely exclusively upon economic incentives to solve problems of such complexity, the widely recommended policy of bringing private costs into conformance with social costs by such measures as internalizing wastes, taxing polluters and charging for emissions merits much wider experimentation than it has received. But, beyond the potentially major role to be played by economic incentives, there is growing acceptance of the need to reconcile economic, social and environmental objectives by direct intervention of the public sector through comprehensive planning. This development is especially evident in proposals in the United States for greater involvement of federal and state agencies in land use planning which has traditionally been left to local governments.

Finally, in response to increasing doubts about the efficiency of conventional regional development schemes to aid the impoverished and to control pollution, regional planners are beginning to adopt more realistic planning concepts and models which deal not only with gross economic benefits, but also with the effects of alternative forms of development upon the interregional, intersectoral distribution of employment, government expenditures and revenue and pollution. These models are emerging partly in order to permit citizens of local regions to participate actively in decisions about the development processes which profoundly affect their lives and to identify the full range of development options open to them. Especially important are alternatives to the traditional industrial development syndrome which can better permit regions to achieve broad socio-economic development objectives with minimal damage to the environment.[1]

These recent developments suggest that there has never been a greater need, nor indeed a better opportunity, to design a comprehensive national policy on regional and urban development.

John H. Cumberland
College Park, Maryland
June, 1973

1. John H. Cumberland and Robert J. Korbach, 'A Regional Inter-industry Environmental Model,' *Regional Science Association Papers*, 1972 meetings, forthcoming.

Contents

Preface by the Director of UNRISD vii

Preface by the Director of the Regional and Urban Studies Program of Resources for the Future, Inc. viii

Acknowledgments xi

Chapter I *A conceptual framework* 1

Chapter II *Issues in U.S. regional development experience* 6

Introduction 6
Is aid to lagging areas necessary? 6
Aid to places vs. aid to persons 10
Regional economic development vs. alleviation of poverty 12
Relocation of persons vs. relocation of jobs 13
Equity vs. efficiency 14
Concentration vs. dispersion of regional assistance 15
Small regions vs. large: Defining the appropriate region 16
The issue of planning 17
The nature of aid 20

Chapter III *Infrastructure for regional development: The era of internal improvements* 21

Introduction 21
A national system for regional development 24
Canals 28
Introduction 28
Programs 29
Evaluation 32

Railroads and the advent of a new system of technology 33
Introduction 33
Objectives 34
Programs 35
Evaluation 39

Chapter IV *Land grants and land use in U.S. regional development* 43

Introduction 43
Values 43
Objectives 45
Issues 45
Programs 47
Evaluation 53

Chapter V *River basin development* 55

Introduction 55
The Tennessee Valley Authority experiment 57
The Ohio River Basin 61
The Potomac River 62
Evaluation 63

Chapter VI *Urban development* 64

Chapter VII *The Area Redevelopment Administration* 71

Introduction 71
Defining the region 72
Planning: The Community Overall Economic Development Program 74
ARA commercial and industrial loans 76
ARA loans and grants for public facilities 77
Manpower training 78
Evaluation 79

Chapter VIII *The Economic Development Administration* 82

Introduction 82
The program 82
Evaluation 87

Chapter IX *The Appalachian Regional Commission* 90

Introduction 90
Objectives 90
Issues 92
The program 95
Evaluation 101

Chapter X *Other multi-state regional commissions* 104

Introduction 104
Values 105
Objectives 105
Issues 106
Programs 111
The Ozarks Regional Commission 111
The Four Corners Regional Commission 112
The Coastal Plains Regional Commission 112
The Upper Great Lakes Regional Commission 114
The New England Regional Commission 115
Evaluation 117

Chapter XI *The special case of Alaska* 119

Chapter XII *An empirical overview of the U.S. performance in regional economic development* 124

Introduction 124
The expansion in personal income 125
The significance of the data 126
Some factors related to regional income differentials 127
Evaluation 130

Chapter XIII *The future of regional development* 135

Introduction: The quality of the performance 135
Some sources of success and failure 136
On the possibilities for improved performance 138
Summary 144

Appendix A *Statistical sources* 147

Appendix B *Research needs* 163

Bibliography and references 165

List of figures and tables

Figure 1 Strategy for the development of the Coastal Plains Region 113
Table 1 Gallatin's proposals for internal improvements, 1808. Summary 27
Table 2 Appalachian Regional Development Program – Authorizations and Appropriations 96
Table 3 Regional income gaps 106
Table 4 Median income of families and individuals, white and non-white 127
Table 5 Percent distribution of families, by income level, by years of school completed, and color of head, 1966 128
Table 6 Unemployed persons, age 18 and over by color and years of school completed 129
Table 7 Incidence of poverty in the total population and the distribution of the poor 131
Table 8 Annual earnings of 4-quarter wage and salary workers, 1966 132
Table 9 Per capita national income in selected countries, 1965 133
Table 10 International comparisons of per capita income 133
Table A-1 Population of the United States 1790-1965 148
Table A-2 United States per capita personal income, by states and regions, 1880-1965, in current Dollars 152
Table A-3 United States per capita personal income, by states and regions, 1880-1965, in constant Dollars (1957-59 = 100) 156
Table A-4 Per cent of total United States population by region and state 158
Table A-5 Population by residence, urban and rural 162

CHAPTER I

A conceptual framework

Of the many reasons for studying regional economic development, one of the most rewarding is the added insight gained about the general economic development process. This brief survey suggests that regional development in the U.S. reflects many of the basic values of U.S. society and many basic forces in U.S. history. This should not be surprising, since at the minimum, U.S. history is a composite of all that has happened in its regions. But a survey of national economic development necessarily omits much of the richness and variety of unique regional experience. To the extent that regional and national values are consistent, they reinforce and strengthen national development. But if regional values diverge excessively, the national structure may be shattered, as in the War of Independence and in the U.S. Civil War. Disaggregation of national experience by space is as essential as disaggregation by time and by industry in advancing understanding of the phenomena involved.

Regional development for the purposes of this study is approached primarily from the economic viewpoint. The term 'regional' is used throughout to refer to any sub-national geographic unit, such as states, metropolitan areas, or multi-state areas. 'Regional development' is treated as one aspect of development and change in these different geographic divisions of the nation. Regional economic development is defined as the spatial aspects of economic development, that is, how national economic development has occurred geographically. The concept of a region is necessarily a flexible one and is defined in terms of size and location of an area which is appropriate to the analysis of the problems involved. Thus for different purposes, the study deals with regions as parts of nations, such as the American West, or as states, or as river basins, or as urban regions which may include parts of different states, depending upon the problem involved.

The U.S. experience in regional economic development, despite its short historical span, has been so rich, complex, and varied that some kind of conceptual framework is essential to provide guidelines for selecting and evaluating the most relevant aspects of that experience. This is especially true of a relatively brief treatise such as this. The conceptual framework is developed in terms of principles, objectives, policies, programs, issues and theory. Programs are regarded as particular sets of actions which are undertaken in order to implement policies. Policies are defined as broad guidelines which evolve in order to achieve goals. Goals, in turn, are derived from basic principles of the society.

Some of these basic beliefs and principles such as the freedom of the individual to pursue life, liberty and happiness are explicitly stated in such official documents as the Declaration of Independence, the Constitution and in published works of political leaders and social theorists. They are also to be found implicitly in the history, literature, and legislation of the nation and its states. Other basic principles of belief, such as fundamental acceptance of technology, change and growth are less explicitly, formally, and legally stated, but appear to be useful nevertheless in explaining the U.S. experience in national and regional economic development.

We begin with a discussion of principles, since these appear to be fundamental value concepts which have tended to persist in U.S. history despite changes in policies, which show more variations over time, and which are even more ephemeral. Indeed, there is reason to question whether some of these uncritically accepted principles have not persisted too long, in forms which are less relevant to changing external events. Reexamination of basic principles in the light of historical change offers opportunities for improving policies and programs for regional development.

A first principle to which most Americans have consistently held as a basic commitment is a firm belief in individual liberty and freedom to pursue individually determined political, religious and economic objectives, so long as this pursuit is consistent with the rights of others. In the economic sphere, this principle has sanctioned and encouraged competition for individual economic advantage, and by extension, the competition among regions for maximum economic growth.

Although the pursuit of economic opportunities was not the only, nor probably the most important, factor in the establishment of the New England colonies, the intensely held theological concepts of the Puritans were entirely consistent with the pursuit of wealth and evolved in the direction of reorienting medieval scholastic reservations about affluence towards a tendency to 'sprinkle holy water on economic success' (Griswold, 1964).

E. A. J. Johnson, in a study of the economic ideas of John Winthrop, has pointed out that the Puritan divines believed that even though man had fallen from an ideal primitive communism, he should yet accumulate wealth for the glory of God. While wealth was not to be idealized, neither was it to be despised. Scholastic objections to charging of interest were neutralized by approval of the need to help one's neighbors by sharing, helping and lending. The groundwork for capitalistic development was further strengthened by exhortations to avoid idleness and to respect property (Johnson, 1964).

A second article of faith in the English speaking colonies was in the right and ability of man to shape his government and his institutions into forms responsive to his pursuit of liberty, freedom, affluence and related goals. This principle and its applications have resulted in a pragmatic, flexible, experimental approach to government without excessive concern for dogma, doctrine, or consistency. It has mattered not if great enterprise involved the intermingling of federal, state, local and private initiatives, so long as the system worked and the objectives were achieved.

A third, and most fundamental belief of Americans (and of Western man) has been in the unquestioned right of man to conquer nature and to use its bountiful resources for his own purposes, and a belief in the ability of man to reshape the natural environment in order to serve his own ends.

And finally, man in North America appears to have had virtually limitless faith in the efficacy of science and technology as the appropriate instruments for increasing his control over nature and environment that they might be used to serve human purposes. As a corollary, change has tended to become identified as progress, which in turn has been measured in terms of physical and material indicators of building, construction and production.

These then are four basic values which have strongly influenced all of the regional and national programs which have been surveyed in this study. These basic principles, having gained general acceptance and legitimacy (Boulding, 1967),become embodied in goals which the society adopts in order to implement the principles. The objectives of regional development, economic opportunity, rising incomes, and full employment are almost inseparable from the American principles of liberty and opportunity. However, an important point is that while basic principles of society change only very slowly, the nature of some of the goals may change as development occurs, and priorities then become modified. For example, earlier concern about economic freedom and opportunity have been modified by growing concern about social justice, security, redress of inequities, and the quality of human life.

These goals of regional development in turn are implemented by the programs which are the major focus of this study. The list of regional development programs to be examined here is not exhaustive but represents an effort to cover the major national efforts to encourage regional development, such as the era of internal improvements, development of western lands, urban development, river basin development, and more recent federal programs such as the Area Redevelopment Act, and the Economic Development Act.

It has been noted that within the framework of this study the selection of goals offers somewhat more flexibility and change over time than is the case with basic beliefs, which exhibit much more inertia. Similarly, goals can be served by a wide range of alternative programs (roads vs. canals vs. railroads) so that controversy can be expected to arise over the selection between alternatives. Some of these issues can be resolved through debate, theory, analysis, and compromise. However, when programs conflict with principles and goals, or when programs fail to emerge to service goals, or fail to adjust to changes in the evaluation of goals, social action and conflict may arise to resolve the issues.

For example, as will be noted below, British efforts to block the American drive to occupy and develop the Western lands and other British constraints on development of American resources generated such conflicts that this factor contributed to the final break between the colonies and the Empire. Similarly, the conflict between the basic beliefs in economic freedom, equality of opportunity and justice as contrasted with regional policies and programs based upon slavery led to the Civil War. Failure to implement policies of equal opportunity through effective programs for reduction of inequalities can be expected to generate conflict.

However, even when programs are consistent with basic social beliefs and principles, other serious conflicts may arise unless basic principles can be evolved and be modified in response to changing conditions, new knowledge, and new priorities. For example, new issues appear to be emerging in regional and national development in some areas where programs in support of principles achieve their initial objectives only to find that success has changed their order of priorities.

General affluence in the U.S. has made more visible and more unacceptable the poverty of minority groups. Affluence and achievement of higher education for larger numbers have led many to question the adequacy of affluence as an objective, and to question the costs which have been paid for affluence (see especially Mishan, 1967).

Another major area of emerging conflict between beliefs and reality is the U.S. confidence in the use of technology to conquer nature and transform its resources for purposes of economic development. Growing evidence on the linkages between economic development and environmental deterioration indicates the urgency of attempting to design regional development programs and technological systems to minimize environmental damage. More fundamental review is needed of the belief that the environment can be increasingly exploited without irreversible damage.

Conflict between these traditional values about regional economic development and changing priorities in the U.S. has generated some major unresolved issues, which will be examined in the next section.

CHAPTER II

Issues in U.S. regional development experience

Introduction

The path towards achievement of regional development in the U.S. has been erratic, partly because of conflicts in the identification of objectives but more particularly because of difficulty in resolving some of the major issues which have arisen over how to achieve these objectives. The fact that these issues are still unresolved presents a major challenge to economists and other social scientists to develop and apply relevant concepts and undertake the research necessary to make clear the benefits and costs of alternative regional development policies and programs. Some of these major unresolved issues in regional development are discussed below.

Is aid to lagging areas necessary?

The first major issue to be considered in the debate over regional development is a challenge to the basic assumption that national policy could or should attempt to intervene in the market process in order to assist lagging regions. This debate is waged on grounds both of public policy concerning national priorities and on grounds of economic theory concerning the causes and treatment of regional disparities. The philosophical position of those opposing distressed-area programs has been based upon traditional concern over interference with private enterprise, opposition to extension of federal powers, and rejection of any program hinting of central planning. This general philosophical position, which has been characterized as social Darwinism, was expressed recently in forceful terms by Senator Goldwater, who asserted that the existence of ghost towns, such as those in his native Arizona, were a necessary price to be paid for efficient national development.[1] Opponents of this form of legislation have also

1. For detailed description of this and some of the other issues involved in legislation and programs of the Area Redevelopment Administration, see Levitan, 1964, pp. 23-24.

feared that modest programs of federal aid to local economies might lead to much larger and more expensive programs. The camel's nose argument in this case was a justifiable one, since the history of U.S. regional programs has shown a strong tendency for programs applied locally to be extended eventually on a nationwide basis.

In support of Senator Douglas, the political and philosophical agreement for aid to distressed areas was expressed by the then-Senator John F. Kennedy of Massachusetts who cited the Employment Act of 1946 as authority for the acceptance of the federal government of responsibility to assure full prosperity for the nation.

Accompanying the philosophical debate about the desirability of aid to distressed regions was an economic argument about the causes and remedies for the lagging region phenomenon. The economic counterpart of the philosophical and political opposition to such aid was the position that regional economic development was actually determined by national economic development and hence was a function of the level of aggregate national demand and of regional response to national market forces. The case against federal aid to lagging regions has best been expressed as the theory of national demand.[2]

In the most simple version of this theory, there can be no long-run problem of regional economic distress because competitive market forces will result in optimal spatial distribution of economic activity. Short-run regional unemployment and declining incomes may result from changing demand factors for regional goods or from declining regional competitiveness. However, according to this theory, in the long run, local unemployment and low incomes will either attract in new investment to take advantage of profit opportunities offered by low cost factors of production, or if this fails to happen because the region has other competitive disadvantages, the unemployed will emigrate to areas of greater opportunity and the distressed area will adjust to a lower level of economic activity. Consequently, in this view, distressed areas are those which have been found by market tests to be non-competitive, and efforts to aid them are likely to be both costly and ineffective. The implication of this theory is that while local subsidies to raise levels of economic activity might be justified on the basis of income redistribution, such subsidies are not likely to raise levels of productivity substantially but would probably be required on a permanent basis. Consequently, national economic growth

2. For an excellent discussion of this and the opposing view of the theory of planned adjustment, see G. C. Cameron, 1969a. The author has also benefited from reading an unpublished manuscript by G. C. Cameron, 'Regional Development: The Federal Role,' a monograph submitted to Resources for the Future, Inc., February 1969. For another perceptive analysis, see Edgar M. Hoover, 1969, pp. 343-357.

could most successfully be achieved by encouraging labor and capital to emigrate from lagging regions to areas of high productivity.

Opposed to this theory of national demand as the determinant of regional activity is the theory of planned regional adjustment. The theory of planned adjustment assumes that market processes cannot be depended upon automatically to result in optimal spatial distributions of economic activity, nor therefore to guarantee maximum national GNP. Rather, it is assumed that unnecessary structural unemployment results from such factors as immobility of factors of production, failure to achieve economies of agglomeration and scale, incomplete information, and misallocation of public and private investment. Therefore, it is argued, aid to lagging regions can be justified not only on the grounds of equity and redistribution, but also because if properly administered, it can improve the overall spatial distribution of economic activity and also increase total GNP for the nation.

The logic of the theory of planned regional adjustment rests upon a number of assumptions. Its major assumption is that a disproportionately small share of public and private capital is being invested in lagging areas as compared with large metropolitan centers. The reasons advanced for this are complex. One is that as cities increase in population, above a certain scale the cost per unit of providing public services increases. Costs of water supply, waste removal, and transportation per capita rise sharply. Despite these diseconomies of agglomeration, investment and population may flow into oversized urban communities because many production, investment and consumption decisions are made on the basis of private costs which fail to reflect the full range of social costs (Cameron, 1969a, p. 209). For example, the commuter prefers to drive his private auto rather than to support the cost of public mass transit systems because the private cost of driving fails to reflect fully the costs to society of air pollution, noise, congestion, and encroachment of highways upon other forms of land use.

Another major concern related to excessive size of supercities is that they attract rural migrants whose lack of preparation for urban life results in high social costs, delinquency, crime, drug addiction, urban unrest, violence, and racial tension. It is claimed that excessive migration into cities is subsidized by urban taxpayers who bear the costs of expensive welfare services which attract newcomers from rural areas before they have been prepared for urban life. The implication of these arguments is that by channeling more public and private investment into rural and medium-size communities in order to provide attractive alternatives to migration into large cities, both the rural areas and the cities would benefit and better conditions could be provided in rural or small town 'staging areas' for those who would otherwise be subjected to the sudden shock of urban life.

Contemporary concern about large-scale migration from rural areas into the city reflects to some extent the traditional Jeffersonian reaction against the effects of urban life and belief in the superiority of rural or small town values. However the movement of millions of migrants into urban areas suggests the waning influence of this set of values.

A second major assumption of the planned regional adjustment theory is that some types of private business activity could reduce costs and increase profits by locating in low-cost rural or small town areas rather than in high-cost urban centers. While this is not true of all kinds of economic activity, some of which require urban locations, many firms because of prejudice or inadequate information are unaware of potential advantages of decentralized locations which might result from relative decrease in costs of transporation and communication. Consequently, it is argued, efforts to provide information about the advantages of decentralized locations and programs to subsidize decentralized location decisions could yield net benefits to businessmen and to local economies.

A final assumption is that modest but timely aid to lagging regions can assist them to arrest their decline and thus avoid continuing large-scale public and private costs. This argument, based upon the dynamics of regional decline, points out that the first local symptoms of economic distress often lead to the out-migration of the younger more productive members of the labor force, and simultaneously to a reduction of public spending on vital public services, such as education. These two related factors tend to lead to further cumulative decline in the attractiveness, competitiveness, and adaptability of the local area. Consequently, it is argued, prompt injections of economic assistance can serve to retain the most productive members of the labor force, attract investment away from over-extended cities and preserve the quality of the public sectors and prevent greater future losses by improving resource allocation and spatial distribution to the region and to the nation.

Clearly, neither the national demand nor the planned regional-adjustment argument is tenable in its extreme form. The national demand theory of universal long-run adjustment is refuted by the many regions where low incomes, unemployment, and excess capacity persist over time. Net in-migration may be retarded in distressed areas, but there is often insufficient net out-migration to generate a new equilibrium at acceptable levels of income and employment. Thus while the national demand theory of regional economic adjustment has not been sufficiently supported by empirical evidence to result in a pattern of regional prosperity acceptable to the nation, it nevertheless provides insight into the nature of the adjustment problem.

Similarly, the theory of planned regional adjustment is not acceptable in its extreme form, which would insist that economic decline could be arrested in every region. Changing patterns of national demand and industry location patterns make it highly improbable that every region can remain sufficiently adaptable and responsive to avoid decline. Nor is it probable that the nation could allocate sufficient resources to regional aid programs to underwrite the prosperity of every region, if regions are defined as small local areas.

However, the theory of planned regional adjustment provides useful insight into the problem of how to assist those regions which appear to have a reasonable opportunity for sustained growth.

As the evolution of U.S. regional development indicates, the debate over the national demand versus the planned regional development theory has been valuable in identifying issues and problems. The establishment of regional development programs indicates that the theory of automatic equilibrium of regional development has not been acceptable in the U.S., but the limitations on these programs likewise suggest that the nation has not accepted the idea of the right of every region to expect sufficient assistance for guaranteed economic development. However, the historical tendency in the U.S. to extend programs of federal aid which have been successful in some regions to all other regions suggests that the expectation of universal aid to regional development is a distinct possibility.

Aid to places vs. aid to persons

The issue of national demand versus planned regional adjustment questions the basic need for a regional development policy, as does the related issue of aid to places versus aid to people. Edgar Hoover, quoting the terminology by Louis Winnick of 'place prosperity vs. people prosperity' has argued convincingly that it would be a costly mistake to adopt as an ultimate objective achieving the prosperity of places rather than the only legitimate ultimate objective which is the welfare of people (Hoover, 1969, p. 5, quoting Winnick, 1966).

There are many valid objections which can be raised against the policy of allocating regional development resources in an effort to guarantee the continued prosperity of particular regions, rather than towards the welfare of the people within the regions. The basic issue is the welfare of individuals in any given place.

While regional development programs are often justified upon the humanitarian basis of aiding the needy, there is no guarantee that creating jobs will provide employment for the locally unemployed, if they do not have the required education, skills, and production capabilities. Unless carefully designed, regional aid programs benefit the affluent and the established rather than the needy who serve as the rationalization for heavy expenditures. Spending large sums on new factories and public works is unlikely to benefit the unemployed unless special efforts are made to help them overcome the handicaps which contribute to their initial unemployment: lack of education, training, motivation, health and productivity. A good case can be made that the most effective way to relieve regional economic distress is to invest heavily in human capital through improved programs of education, vocational training, rehabilitation, retraining, health, family planning, relocation assistance and removal of discrimination.

Therefore, in analyzing alternative programs for regional development, it is important to examine in detail precisely how various proposals would affect various occupations in different industries, to examine the employment and revenue needs of particular communities, and to examine the costs and benefits to particular groups.[3]

These problems raise valid questions about the basic rationale for expending public funds to improve economic positions of particular regions, rather than of individuals, families, and groups. The implicit rationalization behind economic aid to regions, but one which has not been extensively stated or rigorously demonstrated in the literature,is that it is somehow more efficient and more economic to assist people by upgrading a region rather than by helping the people directly. Accompanying this is what is probably the more important traditional preference in the U.S. for attempting to achieve objectives and address human problems through the impersonal operation of market forces rather than through direct aid to the individuals in need. As will be illustrated early efforts to provide public land to settlers were based upon manipulations of land prices, interest rates, tract size, and repayment periods before these unsuccessful efforts finally were replaced by the direct gifts of land under the Homestead Act of 1862. Similarly U.S. efforts to aid farmers have traditionally been designed as aid to crops (support prices) which provides bonanzas to large affluent individual and corporate farmers rather than through direct aid to needy farmers as would have been provided under such proposals as the Brannan Plan, which has as yet been regarded as unacceptable.

The conditions for demonstrating the superiority of using public funds for regional assistance in the form of underwriting place prosperity rather than for aiding individuals to overcome limitations on their

3. For one approach, using a model designed for this purpose, see Cumberland, 1966.

productivity are very demanding, and it should not be surprising that they have not yet been met with any degree of rigor in the literature. It would have to be demonstrated, for example, that per dollar expended, aid to a region would generate more net income for needy individuals over a longer period with less offsetting losses to other regions and other individuals than would other types of programs. Thus the case for aid to places would be strongest under certain sets of circumstances, such as where:

1. large amounts of underutilized social overhead capital exist in a region where growth could be achieved rather than in other regions with fully utilized infrastructure;
2. large amounts of unemployed or underutilized private capital in the form of plant and equipment could be put back into production at lower costs than in other regions;
3. large amounts of low income, underemployed or unemployed labor exists which is unlikely to migrate to more prosperous regions;
4. other local factors of production, such as natural resources, currently underutilized, could be developed in the region more efficiently than in other regions;
5. injection of federal aid could reduce the outflow of young people who would prefer to remain in the region and could prevent deterioration in the amount and quality of public services needed to keep the region viable and competitive;
6. injections of modest amounts of federal aid could assist a region to achieve a rate and scale of growth otherwise not attainable which would then permit the region to achieve self-sustained growth.

But these are at best negative, preventative, or permissive reasons for federal aid to specific regions. A more convincing case for federal aid to regions could be based upon a positive program for achieving certain regional and national goals carefully defined under a constructive national policy for regional and urban development. The objectives of such a national program might be directed towards general overall regional development (rather than mere economic development) and positive improvement of the quality of life and environment. This kind of comprehensive approach to regional development will be discussed in following sections.

Regional economic development vs. alleviation of poverty

Closely related to the issue of aid to persons versus aid to regions is the issue of whether regional programs should be designed primarily to alleviate poverty, or to aid local economic development. Although the distinction between these objectives is often overlooked, it remains an important one. It has already been observed that there is no guarantee that aiding local economic development will alleviate poverty since creation of jobs will not necessarily result in employment of the unemployed or the underemployed in a region. On the contrary poverty, unemployment and underemployment are more likely to result from productivity depressants such as poor education, poor health, excessive family size, family and personal problems, inadequate training, and cultural deprivation. Although programs for regional development are often advocated for a region because of the existence of widespread regional poverty, it seems clear that poverty alleviation requires programs for investment in human capital rather than programs for aiding investment in enterprise capital. By the same logic, it is not obvious that programs aimed at alleviation of poverty will necessarily result in regional economic development. Upgrading of human resources and improving the quality of life are worthwhile objectives in themselves, but for maximum contribution to regional development need to be accompanied by creation of job opportunities. However, improvement of education and productivity should also increase mobility, in order to make migration towards jobs in other regions more feasible.

Relocation of persons versus relocation of jobs

Closely related to the debate over national demand versus planned regional adjustment of economic development has been the issue of moving people versus moving jobs. The purely economic analysis of efficiency in factor utilization contained in the national demand theory of regional development emphasizes the importance of labor mobility and migration in bringing the local labor supply into equilibrium with economic opportunity in order to avoid low incomes and unemployment. Consequently economists have frequently urged that any regional development program should include provisions for encouraging and subsidizing migration. However this recommendation has been strongly resisted on the grounds of human cost and political objection. It has been argued that an affluent society should recognize locational preference as an important human value justifying efforts to bring jobs to people. It has been pointed out in response, however, that the decision to accept lower incomes in order to remain in a preferred location of lesser economic opportunity is a perfectly rational tradeoff of income against other values.

Strong opposition to increased migration and labor mobility as a tool for regional adjustment has also been based upon objection to the necessity for young people to leave a region in order to find satisfactory employment, since it has been observed that the youngest and best educated are usually the first to respond to migration pressures. In addition, holders of public office have traditionally resisted policies and programs which would reduce the size of their constituencies. For all of these reasons, the economists' arguments for migration have encountered persistent resistance in the actual design of regional development programs.

This issue of movement of people versus movement of jobs remains an important one still under debate and like many issues, one which in practice tends to result in compromise and accommodation.

Equity vs. efficiency

Another major issue in the design of regional aid programs has been the conflict between the objectives of equity as compared with efficiency. The equity objective requires that priority in aiding regions should go to those regions of greatest distress, in order to reduce the severest economic disparities. This approach has been referred to as 'the worst first' rule. On the other hand, the efficiency objective of generating the maximum amount of economic benefits per dollar expended for regional development requires that priority in aiding regions should be given to those areas where the potential for high productivity is greatest. Unfortunately these objectives are difficult to reconcile, since the poorest and most distressed regions are likely to be those where productivity is lowest, whereas the areas of highest potential benefits are likely to be those where income and employment rates are much closer to the national average. This issue essentially involves the question of whether regional programs should emphasize short-run aid and relief of distress, or whether they should emphasize development and regional transformation.

Like most critical issues in public policy, the issues of regional aid versus regional development is unlikely to be totally resolved in one direction or the other; since both objectives are important, regional development programs have attempted to achieve both goals, despite the conflict between them. However, since total resources available for regional development assistance are limited, hard choices must be made in practice between the equity goal of assisting regions where need is greatest and the alternative objective of investing limited aid funds where the long-run results will be greater. This problem can be resolved only by recognizing the nature of the tradeoff and explicitly deciding how much cost in human welfare in one region should be borne in exchange for increasing economic efficiency in another region.[4] The choice finally is political, not technical.

4. For a detailed analysis of the problem, see McGuire and Garn (a).

Concentration vs. dispersion of regional assistance

Related to but separate from the aid versus development issue is the question of concentration versus dispersion of regional development assistance. It has been noted that there is a strong tendency in the U.S. to universalize programs of federal assistance and to extend them to all regions. This tendency has been operated traditionally in the field of regional development assistance for numerous reasons. First of all, there has been a belief in the fairness of attempting to relieve distress wherever it is found. Secondly, there are strong political incentives to extend aid to the areas of as many office holders and voters as possible. These tendencies have been reinforced by the traditional belief in equality of economic opportunity which has been extended from acceptance of rights of all individuals to the rights of all regions.

However, opposing the forces for widespread dispersion of regional aid is the idea of concentrating assistance in those regions where its results are likely to be more productive and more permanent. This idea is based upon the assumption that widespread dispersion of aid is likely to be wasteful and ineffective. An advanced version of the concentration doctrine is that aid should be concentrated in a limited number of growth points which are to become capable of self-sustained continued growth. A major reason for supporting this view is the belief that if aid is too broadly dispersed geographically, no critical mass or permanent results can be achieved and needs will be created for continued self-perpetuating expenditure of funds without permanent benefits. The growth point argument is that if aid is applied in sufficient concentrations at a limited number of growth points, there will be generated self-sustaining long-run development processes which will benefit both the growth point and its hinterland.

It should be noted that although this argument is usually linked to the argument for placing aid in regions of greatest productivity rather than in regions of greatest need, the arguments are not necessarily identical. Theoretically, if sufficient amounts of aid are injected into growth points, they could be located in regions of high productivity or low productivity.

Although the growth point hypothesis is an attractive one which is enjoying a current vogue, it contains numerous political as well as theoretical problems which in practice have not been resolved. The debate is a continuing one and the traditional approach of generalizing aid programs to all regions has not yielded exclusively to the growth point concept.

A major gap to date in the analysis of regional problems and in the design of development programs is lack of knowledge and understanding of spatial relationships and their relationships to national and regional objectives. One of the most important implications of the growth point and related issues is that it clearly identifies the need for explicit introduction of the spatial variable into economic theory. Analysis of the problem actually involves the concept of the identification of the appropriate region for economic development purposes. Traditional economic theory, which has largely neglected the space variable and spatial interrelationships between economic activities offers little guidance in the analysis of such problems. However, in recent years, increasing attention has been given to regional studies, interregional economic linkages, location theory, regional development, urban transformation, and environmental change. Although these studies are as yet in their infancy, they are beginning to represent an essential addition of knowledge to the traditional social sciences for the understanding of the issues discussed here.[5]

Small regions vs. large: Defining the appropriate region

Limitations in the state of knowledge about spatial relationships and regional economics are also apparent in the issue of defining the appropriate geographic unit for regional development programs. The acuteness of this problem is underlined merely by listing some of the types of regions which might reasonable be considered as candidates for development assistance: rural agricultural areas, rural communities, counties, groups of counties, groups of states, states, urban centers, standard metropolitan statistical areas, and various combinations of these.

At the extreme, a distressed region could be as small as the region of an impoverished individual or family, either his place of residence, or place of work. The smaller the definition of the region, the larger will be the number of distressed regions and the greater will be the variance in levels of well being. Conversely, the larger the unit, the more individual variance will be concealed in the regional averages. In the U.S. there has been a strong tendency to accept the substate county unit as the geographic division to be considered in regional planning. This unit is not completely satisfactory since it varies widely in size and number from state to state, but it has the advantage of being large enough to be a self-governing political unit, and of being small enough, in most cases, to be reasonably homogeneous and can serve as a building block to combine into larger

5. See, for example, Meyer, 1963 and especially Isard, 1959 and 1960, for efforts to carry understanding of regional phenomena beyond economic analysis into a more general regional synthesis of all social science disciplines.

forms of regional units. It is particularly important to be able to combine counties into planning units which are related to special development problems or opportunities, such as a common watershed, agricultural area, natural resource area, market area, or other homogeneous characteristics with which individual counties are too small to cope.

States are obviously important regional development units in the U.S. because of their strong governments and because of their representation in Congress. But for other purposes, states may be inappropriate units to deal with broad regional problems, such as management of estuaries and interstate river basins, air sheds, transportation corridors, multi-state metropolitan areas, and depressed mountain regions, such as Appalachia. Metropolitan areas are highly important regions because they are the focus of many of society's highest priority problems. For some of these problems, sub-units within cities, especially the urban ghettos, are the crucial regions.

For the future, as population, urbanization, and industrialization become more widespread and more intensive throughout the world, and as accelerated communication and transportation increase the linkages and interdependencies between nations, even the nation-state is becoming too small a region for dealing with some types of environmental developmental problems. The U.S. and its neighbors and other nations will find it increasingly necessary to coordinate their regional development planning.

This partial list of reasonable regional units indicates clearly that there is no ideal geographic area but that the selection of the region depends upon the problem and goals involved. This fact has generally been recognized and accepted in the traditionally pragmatic and experimental approach adopted by the U.S. towards regional problems under which programs have been attempted for a wide variety of kinds of regions.

The issue of planning

Another current issue in U.S. regional development experience is the debate over the type of planning which should be undertaken, and what levels of government should be responsible for the planning. This issue arises for a number of reasons. Politically, the U.S. has been traditionally reluctant to engage in central planning, even though events make central coordination and management increasingly necessary in some problem areas. In the field of regional development the issue becomes sharpened because of possible conflicts between national and regional objectives. For example it may appear to be advantageous from the viewpoint of individual states or substate areas to offer tax concessions and other subsidies in order to attract economic activity from other states. Some economists have argued that local subsidies, especially those in the form of wage subsidies, can improve the spatial distribution of economic activity within the nation (see especially Moes, 1962), particularly if used to offset what are regarded as distortions resulting from minimum wage legislation.

But if competition between regions merely reallocates an existing fixed amount of economic activity, that is, if the conditions are those of a zero-sum game, then this particular form of interregional competition for industry may be wasteful from the national point of view. Further undesirable national consequences can result if interstate rivalry takes the form of competitive lowering of standards for resource management, environmental quality, and other non-constructive forms of local competition (Cumberland and Van Beek, 1967. See also Sherman and Willet, 1968 and Hale, 1969).

Some forms of interstate and interregional competition are more likely to be in the national interest than others and this constitutes a major reason for federal planning of regional development, at least to the extent of establishing minimal guidelines and rules of the game which are in the interest of all regions. Recent federal legislation to establish federal minimum standards for water quality and air pollution control are examples of guidelines which most states have endorsed and welcomed, but which would be unrealistic to expect individual states to adopt because of the competitive disadvantage they might suffer.

However the federal programs for regional development to be examined here show that the U.S. has been traditionally reluctant to establish more than general guidelines and policies, leaving the determination of local objectives very much to local communities, and leaving the planning of specific projects essentially to the local governments and to the local businesses which apply for assistance.

Another issue involved in the planning debate has been how much detailed planning beyond traditional economic development is appropriate in regional assistance. It has been argued for example that some regions, such as Appalachia and the urban ghettos, have suffered such cumulative and massive deterioration that extensive regional transformation affecting all aspects of human life and culture are required for them to achieve parity with national averages (see for example, Caudill, 1963).

It is possible to visualize direct specific detailed socio-economic and physical planning for regions and cities which would specify physical design and quantifiable targets to be achieved within a programmed time schedule. While this type of planning has been widely accepted and recognized as essential for private planning for development of communities and new towns, it has not been seriously contemplated in U.S. planning except for limited U.S. experience with detailed physical planning which occurred in connection with the Greenbelt experiments of the 1930's.

Another issue in U.S. regional development programs has been the extent to which national and local planning for this purpose should be coordinated with other federal activities. Coordination of all federal activities for purposes of regional development could be a powerful instrument in affecting the spatial distribution of national economic activity. The federal government is directly and indirectly responsible for the expenditure of a very large portion of total GNP. Furthermore it directly affects the geographic location of major transport networks, public works, federal civilian and military installations and indirectly influences the location of more activity through its regulatory, administrative, and procurement functions.

However, despite the major influence the federal government does exercise or could exercise over the location of much of the total economic activity of the nation, it has no overall policy on regional development. Despite recent programs designed to alleviate regional distress, most federal location decisions are made on the basis of individual federal department or agency decisions. Even military procurement which is currently the largest item in the national budget with minor exceptions is specifically required by law to be made on bases other than regional economic conditions. A study group of independent specialists appointed to appraise this policy concluded that federal procurement was not an appropriate tool to use for influencing regional development, especially since the Congress had not addressed certain critical policy objectives concerning national goals for regional development. A major finding was that production undertaken to meet federal procurement needs tended to occur where labor productivity, skills and regional industrial capabilities were most adapted for this purpose, and attempts to change the locational patterns of procurement were likely to be ineffective and wasteful (U.S. Dep. of Commerce, 1967).

In addition to reluctance to use procurement actions to affect regional development, the absence of any overall regional development policy by the federal government has other implications for local areas. The failure of the federal government, especially the Department of Defense, to coordinate its construction and facilities programs with local government planning and zoning authorities often results in sudden massive impacts of federal installations on local facilities and disruption of local planning, even though the economic impact may be positive and welcome at least to the local business interests. Local expenditures by military and civilian facilities are the equivalent of regional exports and can have a strong multiplier effect upon the local economy.[6]

However, sudden closures of civilian government facilities and military bases and cancellation of procurement contracts can cause sharp downward local multiplier effects. In recognition of this problem, in recent years, the Department of Defense has offered technical assistance through its Office of Economic Adjustment. However, there remain important opportunities to coordinate other federal programs with federal programs for regional development in order to improve the spatial distribution of U.S. economic activity.

The nature of aid

A final issue to be resolved relates to the kinds of aid to be advanced for the purpose of assisting regional economic development. Here again it is only necessary to list some of the many types of aid which might reasonably be considered to suggest the magnitude of the problem. Aid could be given in the form of outright grants, or as loans, or as loan guarantees. Aid could be provided for public programs, or for assistance to private enterprise. It could be advanced for physical facilities, or for welfare and technical services. Aid could be given to labor intensive activities only, or for capital intensive activities.

Similarly, a wide range of issues arises concerning the conditions under which aid might be granted. Aid programs could be financed fully by the federal government or local contributions could be required. There are various degrees to which federal, state, and local approval could be required. The problem of defining eligibility for aid is a critical one. Aid could be administered through an existing agency, through a single agency, or through agencies designated by a central agency. All of these issues have been faced implicitly or explicitly in the history of the U.S. regional development programs to be considered next.

6. For an excellent analysis of local economic multipliers, see Tiebout, 1962.

CHAPTER III

Infrastructure for regional development: The era of internal improvements

> I only know of one means of increasing the prosperity of a people, whose application is infallible and on which I think one can count in all countries and in all places. That means is none other than increasing the facility of communication between men. On this point what can be seen in America is both strange and instructive. The roads, the canals and the post play a prodigious part in the prosperity of the Union. It is good to examine their effects, the value attached to them and the way they are obtained. America, which is the country which enjoys the greatest sum of prosperity that has ever yet been vouchsafed to any nation, is also that which, in proportion to its age and means, has made the greatest effort to supply itself with the free communication of which I was speaking above.
>
> Alexis de Tocqueville, *Journey to America*, 1833*

Introduction

Some of the basic U.S. attitudes and approaches toward regional development were formed early in the history of the nation. It is, therefore, useful to survey some of this early experience, even though a comprehensive view is not possible here.

The basic economic problem of the new nation was how to gain control over its vast resources and organize them into an efficient market economy. The problems to be overcome were formidable. In addition to all of the political, administrative, and international problems faced by a new nation, capital was scarce, technology was primitive, and communication between regions was uncertain. But if the obstacles were formidable, the potential assets and advantages were almost unique in history. The store of natural resources was unparalleled. The low ratio of population to land

* Translated by George Lawrence, edited by J. P. Meyer. London, Faber and Faber, 1959, p. 270.

and other resources offered a powerful incentive to development. The small, homogeneous population, after successfully defying the strongest nation in the world and winning its independence, was united in its goals and values, relatively homogeneous in culture, and relatively free from the conflicts of class, religion, and factionalism which absorbed so much of the energies and efforts of Europe.'Americans, after their long struggle, were united in their acceptance of the principles enunciated in their Declaration of Independence of establishing a democratic government which would leave men free to pursue individual liberty, economic development and affluence. The new nation emerged under exceptionally favorable conditions of time and space. Its geographic isolation protected it from most of the conflicts and wars which plagued Europe, and the age of enlightenment with its advancement of learning was beginning to make powerful new technologies available to facilitate transportation and industrialization in the new society.

Under these circumstances it is not surprising that the highest priority in economic development was assigned to the rapid establishment of improved transportation and communication within and between the states. What in later periods would be referred to as programs to provide public works, construct social overhead capital and create infrastructure were first described in the U.S. as programs for internal improvements. These programs for internal improvements represent the earliest U.S. experience with regional development efforts. Although their relevance to contemporary problems is limited, some of the parallels with current approaches to local development are striking.

It was suggested above that regional development in the U.S. has been significantly affected by some basic principles of the society, including fundamental beliefs in individual liberty, freedom to pursue affluence, belief in the right to exploit nature for the achievement of human goals, belief in the efficacy of science and technology as appropriate means of modifying and mastering the natural environment so as to harvest its riches, and readiness to develop new institutions and novel governmental forms to facilitate the development process. The effect of all of these factors can be identified in the era of transport infrastructure building upon which the nation embarked in order to develop its regions and knit them together into a market economy which would serve the purpose of permitting regional and industrial specialization, achieving economies of scale, providing access to new resources and to new markets, and in general raising productivity and expanding the scale and rate of national and regional economic development. However, these elements of regional and national economic development throughout the nineteenth century were accompanied by additional factors which still very much affect contemporary thinking about regional development problems. Two of the most important of these factors are the development of vigorous competition between regions for economic development, and the readiness to adopt vast new technologies including the acceptance of the total systems needed to support them. The evolution of these ideas clearly emerges in U.S. efforts to develop its transportation infrastructure.

The need for programs of internal improvement for the support of regional development goals was widely accepted as an important priority in the early history of the nation, but many issues arose over the design and choice of alternative programs. A major issue was the appropriate role of planning to be involved, and the proper governmental level for coordination of planning. Men like Albert Gallatin and John Adams believed that a strong national plan was necessary in order to avoid wasteful duplication and to assure efficient achievement of specified objectives. The oppositve view was represented by states' rights proponents primarily in the South who opposed a strong federal presence on political grounds and believed that regional development could best be administered at the local level. Many opposed planning in principle and believed that the free play of competitive market forces would result in optimal economic benefits.

Closely related to this debate was the issue of the approprate choice of institutions and financial methods for funding the internal improvement programs: federal, state, local or private. Another related issue was concentration vs. dispersion of development efforts. There was also debate over priorities and alternatives in the choice of programs and projects for internal improvements, some factions preferring turnpikes, some canals, and some railroads. These issues remained issues because no single generally accepted resolution emerged. On a pragmatic experimental basis, a rich variety of schemes for internal improvements was attempted throughout the regions of the U.S. Although the fervor for internal improvements was often rationalized on the basis of national security and political unity, and was even vested with the aura of altruism and patriotism which has so often been used to sanctify schemes for economic gain, the one objective these projects had in common was regional economic development.

In the contemporary debate and discussions about internal improvements, implicit theoretical arguments may be identified, some of which are surprisingly consistent with recent theories of regional analysis, public finance, and welfare economics. The expenditure of public funds for transportation and communication projects was partially justified on the basis of contemporary theories about public goods. It was pointed out that proposed programs involved large-scale projects whose benefits would exceed their costs, but which were too large for individuals or small groups or isolated regions to finance.

It was assumed that internal improvements (or social overhead capital or infrastructure as they would be called today) would contribute to national economic development by making it possible to increase regional specialization and division of labor. This, in turn, could be expected to lead to a dynamic process of growth through regional multiplier effects resulting from expansion of the local export base. Indirect benefits were expected from putting to work otherwise unemployed resources. The growth of urban concentrations was expected to lead to particular economic benefits, in the form of what today would be referred to as economies of large-scale production, external economies resulting from the agglomeration of complementary activities, and from expansion of local market size to levels making import substitution possible.

Although neither the early proponents of internal improvement nor the economists of the period developed their arguments formally in these terms, businessmen and political leaders often showed an awareness of the major economic implications in planning and executing their programs.

A national system for regional development

Early U.S. programs for regional development were based upon the concept of relating economic development to construction of national roads and canals. The first notable achievement of this policy was the construction of the National Road, which provided a link between the Atlantic Coast and the Ohio Valley. Congress authorized a survey for the Road in 1806, and construction began in Cumberland, Maryland in 1808. The Road eventually linked Cumberland with Wheeling, West Virginia on the Ohio River, Columbus,Ohio, and finally with Vandalia, Illinois in the 1850's (Dillard, 1967, p. 321).

One of the earliest and most impressive systematic approaches to planning for U.S. regional development was prepared by Albert Gallatin (Reprint, 1968), Secretary of the Treasury to Thomas Jefferson (1801-1809) in his *Report on Public Roads and Canals* in 1808.[1] Even as early as this period, the federal treasury was regarded as a rich source of subsidies for the endless list of projects for roads and canals in the various states. However, because John Quincy Adams, then a U.S. Senator, regarded political favor-trading as a dangerous and costly misallocation of resources and drain of public funds, he demanded a systematic national survey and plan as the price for agreeing to federal expenditures for local improvements. Adams' proposal was for a regional development program based upon national objectives. The program was to be financed by a

1. For an excellent account of the era of internal improvements, see Goodrich, 1960.

continuing revolving fund obtained from the sale of western lands which would also achieve the objective of pushing forward the frontier.

The result of Adams' grand design was Gallatin's *Report*, based upon a comprehensive study of national transportation needs and of alternative methods for meeting these needs. This remarkable study compares favorably in analysis and persuasion with many contemporary proposals for federal programs on regional development and incorporates some of the elements of recent PPB (Program Planning and Budgeting) approaches.

Gallatin began his report with a general proposition which can be interpreted as including an early benefit-cost model and the idea of indirect benefits:

It is sufficiently evident that, whenever the annual expense of transportation on a certain route in its natural state, exceeds the interest on the capital employed in improving the communication, and the annual expense of transportation (exclusively of tolls,) by the improved route; the difference is an annual additional income to the nation [provided the improvement is made].[2] Nor does in that case the general result vary, although the tolls may not have been fixed at a rate sufficient to pay to the undertakers the interest on the capital laid out. They indeed, when that happens, lose; but the community is nevertheless benefited by the undertaking. The general gain is not confined to the difference between the expenses of the transportation of those articles which had been formally conveyed by that route, but many which were brought to market by channels, will then find a new and more advantageous direction; and those which on account of their distance or weight could not be transported in any matter whatever, will acquire a value and become a clear addition to the national wealth.

Gallatin presents cost estimates for each of the projects proposed but does not offer detailed estimates of expected benefits. However an appendix by Robert Fulton does present some specific benefit and cost estimates. In fact, Fulton, an ardent advocate of the superiority of canals over turnpikes, provides an excellent early example of two persistent strands in thinking about U.S. regional development. One is the eagerness to adopt newer and more complex technologies. Another persistent tendency is to assume that a system which is appropriate in some regions under some circumstances should be universally spread throughout the nation. In fact, Fulton makes proposals for extending canals even over mountain ranges, and concludes his statement with a quotation from his letter to the Governor of Pennsylvania on a complete national system of canals that:

2. Brackets added.

canals should pass through every vale, wind around every hill, and Bind the whole country together in the bonds of social intercourse (Gallatin, 1968, p. 123).

Similar enthusiasm and advocacy have been brought to bear subsequently on proposals for railroads, highways, air routes, and can be expected, no doubt, for travel in space. By contrast, Gallatin's proposals were modest though comprehensive. He offered a specific identification of national objectives which were to improve communication and to settle the West, and he based this upon a statement of principles.

No other single operation, within the power of government, can more effectually tend to strengthen and perpetuate that union, which secures external independence, domestic peace, and internal liberty (Gallatin, 1968, p. 8).

Gallatin based his report upon detailed studies of the geographic, historic and engineering problems involved. He developed his national plan for transportation in relation to the total U.S. budget and other priorities, proposing an annual expenditure rate of $2 million for ten years out of expected surplus (Goodrich, 1967. See also Goodrich *et al.*, 1961).

Basing his proposals upon a geographic feasibility study which was impressive for its day, Gallatin recommended a comprehensive system of transportation routes from north to south as well as east to west. The north-south system included both turnpikes and an inland waterway which would make maximum use of existing natural bodies of water efficiently interconnected by canals. The east-west transportation was to be provided by connecting eastern and western rivers by means of a system of canals and turnpikes. The major goal of this program was to overcome the physical barriers to development imposed by the Appalachian mountains. The Appalachian problem in somewhat different form still plays a major role in U.S. thinking about regional development 160 years later, as will be discussed in Chapter IX.

His system, designed on the basis of efficiency, skillful linkage of natural and man-made facilities, and an implicit national benefit-cost analysis was to be financed by a recommended expenditure of $16.6 million based upon the requirements of the system rather than upon any particular apportionment among the states involved. However, in a realistic appraisal of the political factors involved, Gallatin proposed that an additional $3.4 million 'justice and policy' fund be appropriated in order to aid those states not benefited by the basic plan. Details are given in Table 1.

Table 1. *Gallatin's proposals for internal improvements, 1808. Summary*

Objectives	*Projects*	*Costs in $*
I. North-South Transportation along Atlantic Sea Coast	1) Canals opening inland navigation for sea vessels from Massachusetts to North Carolina	3,000,000
	2) A great turnpike from Maine to Georgia	4,800,000
	Sub-total (1 + 2)	7,800,000
II. East-West Communication across mountains between Atlantic and Western rivers	3) Improvement of four great rivers including parallel canals	1,500,000
	4) Four first rate turnpike roads from those rivers across mountains to four corresponding western rivers	2,800,000
	5) Canal around the falls of the Ohio	300,000
	6) Improvement of roads to Detroit, St. Louis and New Orleans	200,000
	Sub-total (3 — 6)	4,800,000
III. Inland navigation between the Atlantic coast, Great Lakes and the St. Laurence	7) Inland navigation between North River and Lake Champlain	800,000
	8) Inland navigation by canals from North River to Lake Ontario	2,200,000
	9) Canal around the Niagara Falls opening sloop navigation from Lake Ontario to upper lakes	1,000,000
	Sub-total (7 — 9)	4,000,000
	Sub-total (1 — 9)	16,600,000
IV. Provide local internal improvements in transportation and communication for those regions less directly benefited by the major projects	10) Roads and canals	3,400,000
	Aggregate (1 — 10)	20,000,000

Source: Compiled from Albert Gallatin (1808, Reprinted 1968).

Although work on the program was delayed by the War of 1812, eventually the entire program was completed very much as originally proposed by Gallatin. A further contemporary note is provided by the fact that John C. Calhoun who supported the plan as a way of binding together the nation with what he regarded as a perfect transportation system and of reducing sectionalism also argued that the network was needed for defense purposes.

The ultimate completion of the elements of Gallatin's proposal demonstrated the high quality of his planning of the geographic and engineering aspects of his recommendations. However, his report dealt less thoroughly with the legislative, financial, and administrative aspects of the problem, and eventually the states had to provide much of the financial resources needed. However, Gallatin recognized the probable need for mixed modes of financing the internal improvements, and this pragmatic approach has become a permanent aspect of the U.S. approach to regional development.

In many ways the Gallatin *Report* represented the high point of an era of national projects which came to a close with the presidency of Andrew Jackson (1829-37) and the emergence of an era of states' rights. Powerful southern states opposed the tariff and tax burdens needed to finance internal improvement when they already had extensive river systems adequate to the needs of their plantation economies. The concept of regional planning based upon a national plan for regional development became overshadowed by forces of sectionalism and interregional competition for growth and development.

Canals

Introduction. There has been a strong tendency in U.S. history for programs which are successfully implemented in some regions to be rapidly adopted throughout the nation. This was the case with internal improvements. The demonstrated success in accelerating economic development of the National Road and of the transporation system visualized in Gallatin's proposals generated strong demands throughout the States for investment in transportation infrastructure as a spur to regional development.

However under the presidency of Andrew Jackson (1829-1837) there emerged an age of state supremacy and constitutional objection to federal interventions such as the tariff and federal taxing power necessary to continue a national program of internal improvements and regional development. This was a period of ascendancy of the South, having a plantation economy which could function adequately in most regions using existing rivers, especially the Mississippi, for transporation. Consequently though there was no diminuition of concern with national policy of pursuing economic development principles and promoting economic development programs, changes in national policy shifted major responsibilities for these programs away from the national government.

Unlike the case of Great Britain, very few large transport projects were fully financed by private entrepreneurs. The distances to be covered and the obstacles to be overcome were in general too great to yield to the limited amounts of capital, organization, and experience which could be brought to bear by individuals or even by joint stock companies. With the role of the federal government greatly diminished, the major burden fell upon state and local governments. However, this shift was never total or complete, and pluralistic combinations of federal, state, local, and private programs emerged, setting precedents for subsequent U.S. thinking about regional development. The emergence of combined public and private initiatives for investment in transport infrastructure was strengthened by intensive regional competition for economic development. The spirited regional competition for economic development was based upon many factors ranging from visionary and altruistic idealism about local progress, to crassest provincial boosterism, through sophisticated analysis of the cumulative economic advantages of an early start.

Programs. The Erie Canal, completed in 1825,introduced the short but intensive period of canal building in the U.S. Making effective use of favorable natural water systems, the Erie Canal connected New York City on the Atlantic coast with the midwest via the Hudson River and the Great Lakes. The economic payoff of this investment was dramatic. Before its completion, the cheapest means of transporting freight to the West was via the National Road, at a rate of $.25 to $.50 per ton-mile. The freight rate on the Erie canal was $.005 to .01 per ton-mile or about 2 percent of the overland route (Dillard, 1969, p. 323), resulting in large transport savings, even though the water route was longer. The canal was financed by the State of New York at an original cost of $7 million. Even with later additions raising total costs to $78 million, it earned large profits until railroad competition began to reduce its long-haul advantage in the 1850's. The opening of the canal in 1825 linked a major industrial port with a resource-rich hinterland, and confirmed the advantage of New York over Philadelphia and Boston, which these earlier competitors were never again be able to match in terms of quantitative growth.

The success of the state-financed Erie Canal quickly led to an era of competitive canal building throughout the nation along the lines which were beginning to characterize U.S. development theory and practice. The demonstrated capability of the new system to earn large profits and to spur regional development led to the competitive mobilization of capital in other regions. The eagerness of investors to respond in other regions generated experimentation with a wide range of financial and administrative arrangements for canal building involving various combinations of national, state, municipal, and private participation. The success of the Erie Canal opened the door to European capital markets.

The profitability of the Erie Canal, which had been financed by the state of New York attracted the interest of private investors as well. In Maryland, a canal along the north bank of the Potomac from Georgetown westward had been begun by the Potomac Company (1784-1828), in which George Washington had been active. This company was reorganized as the Chesapeake and Ohio Company. Both the economic and engineering objectives of the project were carefully formulated. Its goals were to provide an all-weather route from the Atlantic coast to Pittsburgh for boats capable of carrying 50 barrels of flour (Goodrich, 1960, chap. 3).

While the C & O Canal was organized for private profits its promotors had no ideological objections to the use of mixed enterprise in raising money. In order to raise capital to finance their scheme, the promotors appealed both to the hopes for profit by individual investors, and to the State's sense of rivalry and economic competition with other coastal states in establishing trade routes with the interior. Participation by Maryland as a partner in economic enterprise was rationalized as in the case of other states on the basis that successful competition with other states would result in lowering taxes, improving education, increasing land values, improving business, and in achieving other objectives which have a thoroughly contemporary ring.

At the outset of the Maryland program, it was said, everyman dreamed that he was about to reach a new El Dorado free of debt and taxes; an early leader of the movement for internal improvements in Tennessee declared that they would yield a clear revenue sufficient to fill her treasury and support her civil list, as well as to provide extensively for the education of her youth; and all these without taxes on her people (Goodrich, 1960, p. 273).

Unfortunately, the results did not often equal expectations. When states assume the role of entrepreneurs, they run risks of losses as well as of profits, and a number of factors converged to make the states and their creditors losers in the case of the C & O Canal. At the same time that commitments were being made to embark upon construction of this massive transportation system, a new technology was emerging in the form of the railway system, which was in many ways superior. As construction began on the C & O Canal in 1828, Baltimore interests began the construction of a rail line from this city westward towards Wheeling paralleling the Canal for part of its route along the Potomac River. While the Railway reached Cumberland in 1842, the Canal was not completed this far until 1850. Here construction ended, while the Railroad was extended to Wheeling on the Ohio River by 1853 (Dillard, 1969, p. 323). Although the Canal carried much freight, especially coal eastward, it was never a financial success, and the state of Maryland eventually defaulted on its improvement bonds (Goodrich, 1960, p. 273).

A number of factors in addition to the more advanced technology of the railroad contributed to the financial failure of the Canal. One factor, ironically, was the excellence of its design, which called for 'timelessness' of construction, resulting in heavy expense and long delays necessary to meet its specifications. Another factor which added to the problems faced by the Canal was that the state of Maryland, unlike New York State in the plan for the Eric Canal, or the U.S. in Gallatin's report, had no one consistent overall state plan and set of priorities for transportation and regional development. The State dispersed aid through sale of improvement bonds in indiscriminate and inconsistent fashion, supporting the development not only of the C & O Canal, the Baltimore and Ohio Railroad, but also the Chesapeake and Delaware Canal, the Western Maryland Railroad, and numerous other schemes for internal improvements.

Unfortunately, these various projects did not add up to a comprehensive, consistent transport system, but in some cases, notably that of the C & O Canal and the B & O Railway they were in actual competition with one another. In contrast the promotors of the Baltimore City-sponsored B & O Railway, who had a single well planned transport objective in mind, and who also received state aid for their project succeeded in retarding the development of the C & O Canal, thus contributing to the eventual default of the State on its internal improvement bonds. Growing public skepticism and disillusionment about public involvement in mixed enterprises led to increasing inabilities of the State to impose sufficient taxes to finance the extension of programs and to service the heavy level of debts incurred. Civil War action along the Canal contributed to its final bankruptcy, though it continued to haul freight until major flood damage occurred in 1924.

In 1938 the Canal was sold to the Federal Government. Since then it has been partially restored and included in the National Park Service, providing unique recreational resources for the region of the nation's capital. Further efforts are continuing to acquire additional land and establish the area as a National Monument. It does not appear to be entirely unreasonable to expect that the eventual value of the canal for recreation and open space in an urban area may far exceed its original value for the traditional economic purposes of providing low cost transportation and opening the West to development.

Despite the outstanding success of a few canal systems such as the Erie in New York, and canals in Georgia, which were planned for coordination with the railroads in a single consistent system, the hasty and ill-planned rush to adopt the canal system indiscriminately in most other states resulted in the loss to public and private investors of millions of dollars and the corresponding misallocation of resources on a monumental scale. In Virginia, an estimated total of $55 million was spent on scattered local projects which never succeeded in the objective of piercing the Appalachian barrier. Experience in the Carolinas was similar (Goodrich, 1960).

Goodrich estimates that before the Civil War, the total U.S. public investment in internal improvements was $432 million, of which the states provided $300 million, local governments $125 million, and the federal government $7 million. The total investment in canals is estimated at $195 million of which 70 per cent was provided from public sources.

Evaluation. It is not possible here to evaluate the overall effectiveness of public and private investment in canals, though some fascinating and challenging research opportunities remain to be investigated. Canals played a major role in contributing towards regional development by lowering transport costs, opening new markets and extending the scale of existing markets, increasing the opportunities for regional specialization, by providing access to new resources, and by generating regional economic multiplier effects both in the construction stages and in the operating phases of the canals. The major beneficiaries of the canals were not in all cases those regions or individuals which bore the major costs. In many instances, the direct revenues of the canals failed to cover the costs of construction and operation. However, while the financial costs of the projects were probably a reasonable measure of the total economic and social costs involved in canal building, the canals undoubtedly generated many indirect benefits in terms of national and regional development which were not fully measured by the revenues earned. The consensus of scholars who have studied the era is that the overall direct and indirect benefits of the U.S. canal systems exceeded their costs. As De Tocqueville observed, Americans were no longer condemned to 'crawl along the outer shell' of the continent (Goodrich *et al.*, 1961).

The waste and misallocation of resources appear to have been greatest in those states such as Virginia and the Carolinas, where public aid was granted indiscriminately on a large scale on the basis primarily of political pressure and where there was no overall state transport development plan based upon a functional, interconnected system. Waste was great where there was no clear view of reasonable goals to be sought, nor of attempted weighing of the costs to be borne against the benefits to be expected. Allocation of economic resources on the basis of political pressures as well as economic efficiency is not necessarily undesirable. However, in the case of canals which begin nowhere and end nowhere in order to please rival legislators in the use of state funds, benefit cost ratios are likely to be low.

In many instances, the individual state was a suboptimal unit for transport planning in any event, especially where interstate waterways, mountain systems, and other geographic features were involved. Even state plans, where they existed, were no substitute for a national plan, such as Gallatin's when interstate coordination was essential to the efficient design and operation of a transport and regional development program.

While it is clear that canals contributed much to U.S. national and regional economic development; it is not clear to what extent further development and improved planning of the canal system would have advanced the development process. There are inherent limitations in the flexibility and adaptability of the canal system. It began with simple improvement of natural waterways and even at its most advanced stage of development depended heavily upon the favorable proximity of navigable rivers for water supply and interconnections. Cost of construction and lock building was high in unfavorable terrain, and the supply of favorable routes was limited. Carrying capacity was also limited, as was speed. Availability of adequate terminal and turn-around facilities was also a constraint. Thus, despite the expenditure of millions in public and private funds in a burst of canal construction beginning in about 1817, within a few decades the movement ended as the nation adopted newer, more costly, more efficient and far-reaching techniques for accelerating national development and the regional development upon which it depended.

Railroads and the advent of a new system of technology

Introduction. The rapid adoption of railroad technology opens a new chapter in the history of U.S. regional development and demonstrates further evolution of the policies and programs involved. Widespread confidence in the superiority of a more complex technology led to extensive construction of railroads in advance of freight requirements and in anticipation of economic development. Investment in recently completed canal systems was abandoned or rendered obsolete by parallel competing rail lines. The economy and the society readily embraced a complex massive new technology with all of its supporting systems and willingly wrote off much of previous investment in canal systems.[3]

3. De Tocqueville reports an early U.S. observation on planned obsolescence and technological change in quoting a former minister to Mexico, Mr. Poinsett: 'We are

Further ingenuity was applied to the problem of devising new corporate institutions, financial instrumentalities and mixed governmental forms for channelling vast economic resources into railroad construction. In contrast to the quality of the engineering and technical planning, the development of overall national and regional policy planning was sporadic, primitive, and inconsistent. There was general acceptance of the need to settle the West and aid economic development, but no national Gallatin plan for the railroad era was attempted. The result was often conflicting competitive factional rivalry between regions and the waste of resources.

Objectives. Despite the waste, corruption, and lack of planning which characterized much of the early experience with state and locally subsidized rail construction in the U.S., there was evidence to support the view that railroads could serve as powerful instruments of regional development and national unity. There has always been a strong tendency to assume that what succeeded on a small scale in some region should be extended on a large scale to other regions. And although the nation appeared unwilling or unable politically to raise enough revenue through the painful process of taxation to pay for internal improvements, flexible and adaptable governmental policies and administrative programs were devised for achieving the objectives sought.

The major national objectives were to settle the new lands, push the frontiers westward and advance economic development through expansion of the market economy, resource exploitation and regional specialization. The national policy of encouraging internal improvements, especially transporation systems, appeared to be necessary if not sufficient for achieving the goal. Implementation of the policy through dependence upon state, local and private initiatives resulted in some local achievements but was clearly inadequate to provide a national transport network. The need for identification of national priorities and guidelines became more evident as local efforts so often ended in suboptimal systems, waste, corruption and default. The policy which eventually

always expecting an improvement to be found in everything. And in fact that is often correct. For instance I asked our steamboat builders on the North Bank a few years ago why they made their vessels so weak. They answered that perhaps they might even last too long, because the art of steam navigation was making daily progress. In fact these boats which made 8 or 9 knots, could not, a little time afterwards, compete with other whose construction allowed them to make 12 to 15 knots.' *Journey to America*, 1959, p. 111.

evolved in order to provide a national rail transport system without actually imposing taxes to finance it was to rely on private enterprises for building the system by transferring to them very large subsidies in the form of public lands.

National objectives were defined only in the most general form: to develop a transcontinental rail system. The policies adopted in order to implement this objective were to rely on private investors to design and operate the system, to finance the system through subsidies in the form of grants of public lands rather than through taxation, and to rely heavily on private decisions and local government preferences for determining actual routes to be followed.

Between the period after the War of 1812 and 1850, the controversy over the extent of national planning appropriate for transportation systems was resolved in terms of the withdrawal of the federal participation in favor of state and local efforts. Disappearance of the federal surplus and reluctance to impose national taxes reduced the enthusiasm for a national transportation program. The supersedence of Gallatin's canals by railroad technology caught the nation without any clear set of plans for controlling the new technology and shaping it to serve national objectives, nor did the nation have a clear set of priorities for shaping regional development of the western lands. The planning which did occur was done by combination of state and private interests, largely upon the basis of local patriotism and interregional competition. The railroad promotors exploited the local competitive spirit by extracting large payments from communities which bid for rights of way, resulting in system designs which were suboptimal and wasteful. In many instances the mixed public and private enterprise resulted in corruption, with the public bearing costs and risks and promotors enjoying the profits. Unprofitable lines were often sold to the public at high costs.

This lack of systems planning dispersed and wasted the investment funds available rather than concentrating them in lines which connected growth points and productive hinterlands.[4] The failure to design coordinated systems prevented the achievement of the vast economies of scale of which the railroad system is inherently capable.

Programs. The Erie Canal had demonstrated that a well planned, strategically located canal could open to development a very large region, generating benefits and growth both for the terminus and hinterland. Investors in other regions were eager to apply the lessons learned from canals to the

4. The existence of transportation systems is in itself a necessary but not sufficient condition for the establishment of growth points.

new railroad technology. An interesting comparison of the two technologies and their comparative impact upon regional development is provided by a study of the Baltimore and Ohio Railroad since, as noted earlier, it was begun at the same time as the ill-fated Chesapeake and Ohio Canal, (1828), and paralleled the Canal for much of its distance. Like the Canal, the B & O Railroad was primarily a private enterprise venture, which was heavily subsidized by the public sector. The promoters of the B & O Railroad had very clear objectives in mind, which they implemented with a high level of determination and sophistication. Their purpose was to concentrate upon a single transportation system which would link Baltimore with Pittsburg and the Midwest, making Baltimore City a major industrial center and world port. By concentrating upon this single objective, obtaining adequate financial support from a wide range of sources, discouraging competition from the C & O Canal, and by avoiding political pressures to divert subsidies to other regions, the designers of the B & O Railroad ultimately achieved notable success. They transformed a struggling shipbuilding center on the Upper Chesapeake Bay into a major industrial complex and one of the nation's largest ports.

Recognizing the significance of the Erie Canal transport system in the growth of New York, the B & O promoters were able to obtain extensive subsidization from the City of Baltimore, in addition to the federal, state, and private funds available. Support from the city for the railroad is estimated at approximately $12 million (Goodrich, 1960, pp. 186-190). The railroad had reached Wheeling, West Virginia by 1852, and eventually had connections with St. Louis, Chicago, Philadelphia, and New York.

Rail technology has the characteristic that once lines are in place, the system is capable of moving vast amounts of freight at declining unit costs. The railroad and the port concentrated from the beginning on exploiting the load carrying capability of the B & O in order that the Port of Baltimore might specialize in heavy materials handling so that it could serve the coal mines of the Appalachians and the grain producers of the Midwest. In the present era, the Port of Baltimore is not only a major industrial port, but continues to specialize as a bulk handling and transshipment break point between rail and water shipment.

Although the construction of the B & O Railroad never did permit Baltimore with its emphasis upon bulk movement to achieve a level of economic performance comparable to that of New York City which emphasized value of shipments, the Railroad was a primary factor in making Baltimore a major world port, and in bringing much of the Midwest into the emerging market economy of the nation. A number of factors were involved in the success of the project. It was well conceived from the viewpoint of economic feasibility. Its promotors had a limited set of objectives which they pursued without deflecting their efforts into unrelated programs. They exhibited great skill in mobilizing financial resources from federal, state, local, and private sources. They were able to relate their profit objectives to national interests in internal improvements and to regional interests in geographic competition.[5]

Many states as well as the federal government were reluctant to impose taxes to plan and support coordinated transportation systems but did provide aid by using state credit to issue securities. Conditions varied greatly among states. Far from providing public support for internal improvements New Jersey charged private canal companies for the privilege of building. Ohio in 1837 actually required the state to aid all pikes, canals, and roads under certain circumstances (Goodrich, 1960, pp. 123-136).

By 1850, the Appalachian mountains had been crossed, bringing the Midwest into the national economy, and construction of a transcontinental rail system became a national objective. An era of national subsidy began in that year when an extensive grant of federal lands consisting of 3,750,000 acres was made to the states for construction of a system of railroads. Although there was reluctance to undertake detailed route planning by the federal government, Congress did specify the termini, leaving route determination to local competition. Even during the Civil War, the transcontinental tracks were pushed forward. Although the southern states had urged priority for a southern route, which would have been the cheapest to construct, the War temporarily solved the problem of interregional competition, and the Union Pacific route from Omaha to Sacramento was pushed through with the aid of enormous subsidies. Beginning in 1862 the promotors were given 10 sections of land (640 acres each) per mile plus mortgage loans in excess of $50 million.

Although another act in 1864 had as its objective limiting the federal subsidy to a level just sufficient to attract enough private capital to complete the construction, 20 sections were provided per mile and the federal government was given a second mortgage. The construction of the Union Pacific was promoted by the Credit Mobilier which distributed some shares at little or no charge to members of Congress. With a total investment by the Credit Mobilier of about $4 million, using federal land sub-

5. As is increasingly the case in industrial development, the success of Baltimore in becoming a major bulk materials-handling, industrial port has generated difficult problems for the future. The discharge of heavy metals and other pollutants over long periods is creating a serious environmental threat to the seafood industry and ecology of the Chesapeake Bay and its tributaries. The pressure of a highly autonomous Maryland Port Authority to dredge ever deeper channels to accommodate larger ships threatens to disperse silt and other pollutants over broader areas. See Coulter, 1968.

sidies and federal guarantees to attract loan capital, the promotors cleared profits conservatively estimated at $14-15 million (Goodrich, 1960, pp. 186-189). This pattern of bribery, federal subsidy, low venture capital and enormous speculative gain followed in the case of the Union Pacific Railroad was repeated in the case of the Central Pacific Railroad and helped to establish an unfortunate precedent for subsequent development of U.S. transportation systems.

In many instances, railroad promoters exploited local aspirations for competitive economic advantage by offering to run their lines through those communities offering the highest subsidies for the privilege. In New York, the New York and Oswego Midland Railroad followed a zigzag route between subsidizing towns but was not able to earn enough revenues to avoid bankruptcy. The financial and political power of the railroads often led to corruption, high profits to the promoters, and losses to the bondholding citizens (Goodrich, 1960, chap. 7). Many rail lines were designed to exploit local short-run conditions rather than to serve long-run development goals.

However, the railroads were built and contributed significantly to the regional development of those areas through which they passed. The debate continues over cost effectiveness of the subsidies granted and whether the railroads could have been built more efficiently at lower real cost. Goodrich estimates that the amount of subsidy to railroads eventually reached the staggering total of $62 million plus 129 million acres.[6]

It can be argued that the gift of public lands to promoters was in fact a kind of tax, or that such action imposed an opportunity cost, since if the lands had been sold to the promoters, or turned over to the public, or used for other purposes, taxes might then have been lowered, or the returns used for other purposes. This is a valid point, though those who favored subsidizing railroads through gifts of public lands argued explicitly that the policies followed created new economic values by accelerating economic development. Implicitly they were suggesting that large positive benefit cost ratios were created even after proper evaluation of alternative uses of the lands and of the direct and indirect effects of the alternatives benefits and costs. It has also been argued that the subsidies permitted building the railroads to meet development goals in advance of the effective demand for freight services, and that they otherwise could not have been built.

Opposing views are that without subsidies, an adequate rail system would have developed anyway, that the system as constructed under the subsidies was overbuilt and wasteful, and that lower levels of subsidies

6. Another student estimates the total at 223 million acres. See Ellis, 1964.

and better planning could have resulted in a more efficient system. Although the gifts of land from the public domain appeared to be costless at the time, they later earned the railroads larger profits than were necessary or justifiable. The size of subsidies, regional competition in construction, and small proportion of equity capital offered little incentive for efficiency, and much opportunity for quick profit.

Albert Fishlow has posed serious questions concerning the basic rationale for heavy subsidization of the railroads (Fishlow, 1965). Granting that infrastructure may have limited ability to create growth and diversification, as in the South, Fishlow questions its necessity as a precondition for growth. He advances the argument that railroads would have been built more efficiently without federal subsidies in the U.S., since there was adequate private capital and market responsiveness, ample resources, demographic mobility, and sufficient land, and available demand. In his view U.S. railroads were not risky, developmental ventures built ahead of traffic, necessary as a precondition for regional development, but were built behind demand at great cost to the American public. This is in sharp contrast to the view of the railroads that the land grants and subsidies were successful in getting the job done for the nation, which as a shrewd landlord, received good value for its money (Henry, 1964).

Dillard has pointed out that the minimum figure for the acreage granted to the railroads, 129 million acres, exceeds the combined acreage of all six New England States, plus New York, New Jersey, Pennsylvannia, Delaware, Maryland, and West Virginia. However, he draws an important distinction between the abuses in administering the land grants and the economic principle behind them. The railroads achieved the national purpose behind them of accelerating regional and national development and increasing the value of the remaining public lands. He also points out that the only alternative to private construction of railroads would have been government construction, which may or may not have been better on balance (Dillard, 1967, pp. 223-224).

Evaluation. In many ways, the U.S. experience in utilizing internal improvements to aid the development of its regions and link them together in a growing national economy succeeded brilliantly. The successful adoption of powerful new technologies provided the basis for rapid national economic growth which was widely if not universally shared among the regions. The new transporation system opened new resources for development and encouraged migration of people to the location of economic opportunities. The transportation basis was provided for an industrial economy of unprecedented size and efficiency, and capability for growth.

U.S. society demonstrated a flexible, pragmatic response to the challenge of forming the new, pluralistic institutions necessary for mobilizing the vast amounts of capital required to finance the new technologies and for administering their construction and operation. As De Tocqueville noted in *Journey to America:*

> The American government does not interfere in everything, it is true, as ours does. But where great works of public utility are concerned, it but seldom leaves them to the care of private persons; it is the State itself that carries them out; the great canal joining the Hudson to Lake Erie was made at the expense of the State of New York; that joining Lake Erie to the Mississippi is the work of the State of Ohio; the canal joining the Delaware to Chesapeake Bay is an undertaking of the State. The main roads which lead to distant places are usually planned and carried out by the States and not by companies.
> But it is important to observe that there is no rule about the matter. The activity of companies, of parishes and of private people is in a thousand ways in competition with that of the State. Turnpikes or toll-roads often run parallel to those of the State. In some parts of the country, railways built by companies fulfil the functions of the canals as main thoroughfares. The local roads are maintained by the districts through which they pass. So then no exclusive system is followed; in nothing does America exemplify a system of the uniformity that delights the superficial and metaphysical minds of our age...
> From this variety springs a universal prosperity spread throughout the whole nation and over each of its parts (p. 272).

In the light of these positive achievements, it might appear to be less than constructive to examine the negative aspects and the mistakes which can be identified with the advantage of hindsight. However, there are important reasons for reevaluating these previous efforts, both because of their similarity to current proposals, and because the magnitude of current proposals is so large that any savings of resources and avoidance of errors can result in very large benefits.

There are also striking parallels between this early experience and current issues before the nation in regional and national development policy that add to the importance of reexamining the historical record. It is only necessary to reflect upon proposals for the St. Lawrence Seaway, the Ohio Canal, interstate highway systems, urban rapid transit programs and other costly programs of regional and national development to appreciate the parallel. All of these programs have regional development implications and all of them share features characteristic of the era of internal improvements. In each of them, Federal funds are declared necessary because private capital is not available in sufficient quantity. The indirect and secondary growth benefits are expected to exceed the amount of the federal subsidy. Creative partnership between public and private capital is said to be required by new conditions. Public safety and national defense are involved. It is asserted that technological change assures progress and the success of the new system once public investment demonstrates its feasibility. Also, if the system appears to be successful in some regions, pressures develop for its spread to all regions.

The U.S. experience with internal improvements for regional transportation systems suggests the most successful projects were those in which widely accepted specific objectives were identified and efforts were concentrated upon particular projects, rather than being dispersed and duplicated. Examples are Gallatin's national system, the New York State Erie Canal system, and the Baltimore City promotion of the Baltimore and Ohio Railroad.

Chances of success were also greater where planning in projects of this kind took place on the basis of large complementary regional units with planning for a total system of productive hinterlands related to focal points for processing and marketing. Gallatin's plan provided for linkage of different transportation systems of canals, natural waterways, and turnpikes. Planning for large integrated systems permitted achieving economies of scale, creating external economies between systems, and achieving regional specialization.

By contrast, a policy of supporting widespread subsidization of internal improvements which had been successful in some carefully planned instances, resulted in waste of resources and loss of investment. Failure to integrate scattered local systems resulted in wasteful interregional competition. Failure to plan for integrated systems, for example, led to use of a variety of railroad track gauges for local systems which could not then be economically linked up.

In some programs, partnership between systems of federal, state, local, and private financing demonstrated that mixed systems could be successful, if carefully planned and closely administered to prevent abuses. But where administrative supervision by public authorities was careless, corruption and failure were extremely costly to the public. Long-term planning over the life cycle of the project was necessary if the public was to recapture its heavy investments. Otherwise promotors captured the profits after the public financed the investment.

In some instances, large percentages of total expenditures on internal improvements were acquired by promotors as profits, and an early tendency was established in the U.S. that even though programs appeared to be designed for national, humanitarian, or idealistic purposes, the primary beneficiaries turned out to be the active, established, well-to-do groups who learned early to design public expenditure programs to operate in their private interests. This system of operation, though perhaps wasteful in some respects, was not altogether ineffective. It was successful in getting programs established and accomplished. It is probably justifiable to provide incentives to those whose assent is necessary for getting programs accepted, and it is in the public interest to reward risk-takers for performing their functions. After all, many schemes were failures, and the entrepreneurs as well as the investors suffered heavy losses. Among the many unsettled public policy issues is the question of what size and what kinds of incentives are most effective for encouraging the success and efficiency of programs for regional development and other objectives.

Among the most important lessons to be learned from this experience is the need for careful identification of goals through benefit-cost analysis, planning in terms of a total system, specific planning for responsible repayment of public funds, and preferably, public participation in profits as well as losses.[7] What is most needed is a concept of constructive interregional competition providing national guidelines for regional programs which will avoid wasteful duplication and lead to improved national prosperity. As the magnitude and relative importance of the public sector grows, and as the costs of new technologies for regional and national economic development escalate, it is increasingly important to develop new models of the public sector appropriate to the evaluation of such competing claims upon the public treasury. Some important new tools of analysis and improved versions of existing tasks are becoming available. They are refinements in benefit-cost analysis, welfare economics, program planning and budgeting systems (PPBS), social indicators, inter-industry studies, and increased awareness of the relationships between economic development and environmental change. It is not always possible to apply these methods in retrospect to historical events, but there is some reason for optimism that these approaches may improve understanding of the issues involved in future regional development problems.

7. See for example the proposals of J. A. Stochfisch and D. J. Edwards (1969) for safeguarding public investment in the supersonic transport aircraft.

CHAPTER IV

Land grants and land use in U.S. regional development

Introduction

One of the major factors which has affected regional development and determined the spatial distribution of economic activity in the U.S. has been land use policy. The problem of land use is also one which illustrates the interrelationships between national values, objectives, action programs, and the issues surrounding them.

Values

One set of values which emerges more clearly in the case of land grants than in the case of internal improvements is concern over the welfare of individuals and families. In most early, and some current,U.S. programs, regional development aid is provided primarily for lagging geographic regions or for distressed industries under the implicit or explicit assumption that somehow needy individuals and families will ultimately benefit. But in the case of its land policy, the U.S. consistently attempted to achieve certain objectives concerned directly with the welfare of individuals. These goals were often circumvented or used as rationalization for other objectives but they remained a constant national purpose.

Basic U.S. principles and values concerning land evolved partially in reaction against the European feudal land practices, partially against British colonial land policy in America, and partially as a new amalgam based upon pragmatism, experience and invention. It has been noted that one of the factors in the U.S. revolution was the futile British effort to discourage strong American pressure for westward migration beyond the Appalachians, in order to protect their interests in the fur trade (Dillard, 1967, pp. 201-202). The colonists also reacted strongly against the feudal land laws of entail, primogeniture, quitrents, and against retention by the Government of vast tracts closed to settlement.

The reaction against these prohibitive and uneconomic constraints led to a strong and positive belief in the basic right of individuals to have access to land, and to have the opportunity to become landowners, secure in their title. Belief in the right of individuals to be owners of property, especially land, was further supported by the philosophical convictions of the colonial thinkers and political leaders. Thomas Jefferson's belief in the rural landowners as the salvation of the new nation is well known.[1] Thomas Jefferson urged that the future of the nation should be based upon the rural freeholder not only as against the urban proletariat, but as against any form of rural tenancy. Jefferson's views as expressed in the Declaration of Independence were heavily influenced by those of the English philosopher John Locke who based man's right to life, liberty and property, on arguments of efficiency and productivity, as well as upon ethics and natural law (Brewster, 1963).

In place of the rigid feudal institutions regarding land tenure, the former colonists were ready to experiment pragmatically with free market concepts of land permitting individual freeholding and the right of free disposal. This legal approach was consistent with economic efficiency which required free exchange, efficiency incentives for individual owners, land consolidation, ease of mortgaging, and mobility of the factors of production. Willingness to experiment with new forms of land ownership, title conveyancing, and mortgaging, as well as with new programs for managing and of disposal of public lands has consistently characterized U.S. land policy.

Another basic belief which has characterized U.S. attitudes to land use and regional development has been a conviction that man could and should conquer nature and reshape his environment to serve his needs and wants. The westward migration and land settlement in the face of an

1. Ironically, it was the Jeffersonian South which to a greater extent than any other region rejected Jefferson's views on freeholding in favor of aristocratic holdings of large tracts which were worked by slaves and tenants. Douglass North has pointed out that in the South, the aristocratic plantation system discouraged investment in human capital and in raising productivity through education, since plantation owners tended to send their children to private schools and failed to support public schools. Also, a high propensity to import led to expenditure leakages out of the South, and plantation exports thus failed to generate the regional expenditure and income multipliers experienced in other regions. Since few inputs were purchased locally for plantation agriculture, the South failed to achieve the sustained regional development enjoyed in other areas having more sophisticated agricultural policies and industrial development (North, 1961).

often hostile nature both challenged and appeared to confirm this fundamental American assumption about proper use of his environment.[2] While the settlers were eager to adopt those contributions of Indian culture such as tobacco and corn which could be exploited on a large scale, it is not surprising that they neglected or rejected much of the basically conservationist value system of the Indian, who himself was regarded as part of a hostile environment to be subdued. These philosophical and economic justifications for occupying the west coincided with and were reinforced by the political and military objectives of occupying the continent and securing the frontier.

Objectives

The values, beliefs, and principles which were generally held in the U.S. concerning land were embodied in specific objectives which were consistently held over time, even though there was conflict between some of the objectives, and priorities changed between them over time. Paul W. Gates (1968),a leading scholar of U.S. land law, has identified four major objectives which have dominated public land policies from the colonial period until the end of the 19th century. They are:

1. To produce revenue for the government and avoid the necessity for raising taxes.
2. To facilitate the settlement and growth of new communities.
3. To reward war veterans.
4. To promote education, establish eleemosynary institutions and contribute to internal improvements through gifts of land.

Swenson (1968) observes that multiple purpose land management and conservation did not emerge as an important objective until much more recent times.

The efforts to achieve these objectives of U.S. land policy were implemented in proposals for various specific programs and acts of legislation, and issues emerged as the result of conflicts between alternative methods for achieving the objectives. The issues were resolved or compromised in the specific programs which eventually were adopted.

Issues

An initial issue emerged over the conflict between the Jeffersonian

2. The basic views of the settlers contrasted sharply with those of the Indians. The original inhabitors of the continent accepted their natural environment and changed it little, both because they lacked technology for massive change, and because they believed in living in harmony with their environment.

objective of getting land into the ownership of small holders and other pressures to make very large grants for special purposes. It has been noted that very large donations of land were given to the states for eventual disposal to finance internal improvements and other programs. Much of this land went to wealthy, powerful individuals and enterprises, and land speculation became a recurrent and troublesome problem in U.S. experience with land policy. Very large blocks of land could be acquired under programs for mineral bearing lands, and timber lands. Conflicts between the objectives of encouraging small land owners to work their own land and the objective of large scale land development for purposes of speculation, mining, timbering, public works and accelerated economic growth have persisted from colonial times until the present.

Issues also arose between the objectives of keeping the prices of public land low to encourage large-scale settlement and equal opportunity, and between the objectives of raising revenue and encouraging increases in land values for revenue and development purposes. Federal objectives of keeping land prices lower for settlers and giving free land to veterans were in conflict with the policies of states, railroad companies, and speculators who were attempting to drive prices upward.

Another important issue was that of federal control as opposed to state and local control. The original 13 states were naturally eager to retain the public lands to the west of them, and the new states of the west wished to acquire the public lands within their borders. This issue was closely related to another problem, the extent to which the disposition, management, and use of public lands should be planned and to what extent a laissez faire policy should be adopted.

In later years, the nature of these issues and conflicts has become modified with changing events, and new issues have emerged. A later issue is complete disposal of public lands as opposed to extensive federal retention of remaining lands. This is closely associated with a related issue concerning lands remaining in the public domain, *i.e.* development versus non-development of public lands. The movement which has been termed the 'new conservation' that has emerged in a nation now heavily populated, widely urbanized, and intensively industrialized, has raised a host of new and urgent issues, as well as sharpening some of the traditional issues. Among the important conflicts are preservation versus use, wilderness versus recreation, and development versus environmental management. These and other issues have been addressed and resolved or compromised in various U.S. programs for land use and management.[3]

3. For more complete treatment, see works cited here and references in Ottoson, 1963. Other major works should result from the comprehensive research undertaken by the Public Land Law Review Commission. See also B. H. Hibbard, 1939.

Programs

The issue of federal versus state jurisdiction was compromised in various ways. The lands to the west of the original colonies were in general administered by the federal government rather than the states to which they were contiguous. However, large acreages of these lands were returned to the states to be used to finance public improvements, education and other public programs. After the proposals by Gallatin for a national program of internal improvements, very little detailed planning occurred at the federal level, although broad, permissive guidelines for use of federal lands were established by Congress. Reluctance at the federal level to undertake detailed planning and to provide close administration of public lands has been a persistent trend in U.S. history. However, the federal guidelines for land policy despite lack of detailed planning were extremely important in dealing with the issues involved.

Although the issue of the small holder versus the large speculator-developer had been theoretically resolved in favor of the family farm, the problem of implementing this goal was difficult. Wealthy, influential, educated, experienced speculators found numerous opportunities to assure that programs adopted to achieve social goals were actually operated for the benefit and enrichment of those in power. Early efforts beginning in 1785 to set minimum acreage of homesteads at 640 acres at $1.00 per acre and requiring full payment within 3 months, but permitting payment to be made with public debt instruments selling at discount, made land acquisition difficult for the settler but easy for the speculator (Dillard, 1967, p. 221). Later efforts in 1796 to cut the minimum acreage in half and double the land price discouraged speculators and farmers alike. Continuing efforts were made to favor the frontier settler over the speculator by pragmatic experiments in varying the terms of credit, size of grants, price of land, and recognitions of squatters' claims. Secretary of the Treasury, Alexander Hamilton, had proposed sale of public land by auction, which would probably have had advantages in terms of raising revenue and achieving efficiency of development, but at the expense of the less affluent settlers.

These early efforts represented attempts to achieve national objectives by manipulating the market processes by varying prices, credit terms, and acreages. In general they were unsuccessful because the market operated to ration land in terms of effective demand given the then-current distribution of wealth and income. The result was to favor distribution of the public lands to the wealthy, the educated, the powerful, and to those who were willing to borrow and speculate rather than distributing land to less affluent settlers. Eventually, it was realized that achievement of the

Jeffersonian objective required direct action programs designed for that purpose rather than reliance upon manipulation of the market mechanism, which tends to aid the affluent.

Finally, in 1862 the Jeffersonian idea of free and equal access to the public domain was most fully implemented by passage of the Homestead Law, under which any citizen could receive free title to 160 acres of land after filing a claim and living on the land for five years (Dillard, 1967, p. 222). This act resolved the cheap land versus public revenue issue clearly in favor of the land distribution objective for those of limited means, and reduced some of the incentives for speculation in agricultural lands. The great achievement of the Homestead Act was that despite the many problems noted here, some 80 per cent of the public lands distributed did become family farms as envisioned by Jefferson and others.

Although the Homestead Law represented an important step forward in the evolution of U.S. policy for land management, serious problems arose from failure to recognize environmental differences in land arising from soil, climate, land cover, mineral content, topography, drainage and other natural features. Treating land as essentially homogeneous rather than classifying and managing it in accordance with its environmental characteristics led to numerous abuses and has been a major defect in U.S. land policy.

Some of the most serious abuses occurred with respect to timber land, grazing land, irrigated lands, and mineral lands. Until 1878, the more valuable timber land in the public domain was priced and treated simply as agricultural land so that speculators were encouraged to acquire it in large quantities at low cost without concern for long-run timber management methods. Excessively rapid disposition of federal timber lands encouraged short-run exploitation, theft of public timber, and damage to the land cover which caused irreversible damage over extensive areas. In addition, poor administration encouraged fraud and corruption in disposal of vast tracts of public timber land at losses to the public of hundreds of millions of dollars (Dillard, 1967, p. 224).

Mismanagement of mineral lands in the public domain also occurred on a large scale. Theoretically, mineral lands were subject to special treatment in the U.S. as in Europe. Again however, reluctance of the federal government to survey, classify, and administer its mineral lands resulted in its sale at agricultural prices. In fact, the administration of public mineral lands was so bad that ores bearing precious metals flagrantly stolen from public lands were actually purchased by the U.S. Treasury (Le Duc, 1963). Not until the twentieth century did federal management of its mineral lands improve, and many abuses still remain to be corrected.

A recurring strand in the history of U.S. land management and regional development has been the rapid adoption of new technology for short-run resource exploitation. The introduction of cheap barbed wire in the latter half of the last century was seized upon in the West in order to fence in illegally millions of acres of grazing land from the public domain. Again, poor administration and poor management were contributing factors. Eventually the flagrance of the grazing land abuses led to prosecution of the offenders and restoration of the lands to the public domain (Dillard, 1967, p. 225).

Failure to classify public land by environmental characteristics and failure to manage public lands in terms of environmental criteria have led to other serious problems in U.S. regional development, especially in the case of the arid lands of the West. Lack of land classification procedures resulted in formation of homesteads which were both too large and too small. The 160 acre pattern, which was reasonably appropriate for the east and midwest was much too small for the sparse land cover of western arid lands, where more extensive cultivation was required. At the other extreme, once arid land was irrigated, 160 acres could support many families.

Despite worthy objectives of reclaiming arid lands, conquering a hostile environment and making the desert bloom, U.S. efforts to achieve regional development in the West through large-scale irrigation have been wasteful and inadequately planned. Much can be learned from a careful study of this experience which should be of value in designing future regional development efforts. The idea of making the desert to be fruitful has been a powerful one, from at least the time of the Old Testament. When allied with U.S. objectives of settling the West and reshaping a hostile environment to serve human needs, it was not suprising that men's imaginations were captured and that vast energies and resources were channelled into what became known as the reclamation movement.

Even John Wesley Powell, explorer, scientist, Professor of Geology, leader of the boat expedition through the Grand Canyon, and founder of the U.S. Geological Survey, vastly overestimated the feasibility of irrigation in the West. He claimed that 100 million acres could economically be irrigated.[4] In attempting to carry out the recommendations of Powell and others for irrigating the West, problems were encountered and a full range of classic mistakes were made and which unfortunately continue to be made, but which should offer guidelines for improving regional development performance in the future.

4. Much of the following material is based upon the excellent study of the reclamation of arid lands by Paul W. Gates, 1968.

Early reclamation legislation in the form of the Desert Land Act of 1877 yielded little settlement, but did transfer vast tracts of land to cattlemen and speculators. The tracts which were most feasible for irrigation were quite early provided with water by private owners and by private enterprise, beginning with the Indians, Mormons, and other early settlers. Their success led to demands that federal irrigation aid be provided elsewhere. Once again, techniques which were successful under certain circumstances led to demands for extensive application elsewhere without careful studies of feasibility. The rationale was a familiar one by now in justifying federal aid for regional development efforts relying heavily upon assumptions of secondary benefits, externalities, scale economies, and the infallibility of technology and engineering.

The result was the Newlands Reclamation Bill of 1902, which provided that all funds from the sale of public lands in 16 western states be deposited in a Reclamation Fund for irrigation works. Creation of the fund put the federal government into the business of planning and administering a program for which it was ill equipped by tradition, training or experience. Unfortunately, the Bureau of Reclamation began to plan large engineering projects which were inadequate for the solution of what were actually complex socio-economic environmental problems. Poorly designed construction schemes resulted in dams which silted up and caused ecological changes such as the spread of Johnson grass. Poor planning and design resulted in water logging and an alkali poisoning of the land.

In addition to environmental problems, serious economic problems were created. Requiring that all funds from sale of western lands be put into a fund which could only be used for irrigation encouraged excessive and uneconomic expansion of irrigation projects. Poor administration resulted in land speculation and wasteful management practice. Early failure to cooperate with other relevant agencies such as the Department of Agriculture and the U.S. Army Corps of Engineers resulted in demands by Congress for reform. Reforms were made, but they were too late, inadequate, and too narrowly conceived. For example, extensive acreages of sugar beets were produced, resulting in the costly use of subsidized water to produce additional acreages of a crop already in excess supply. After World War I, vast acreages of cotton and wheat were planted on irrigated lands while these crops were in surplus. During the Great Depression of the 1930's, while the Agricultural Adjustment Administration was paying farmers to restrict production, extensive new tracts of arid land were reclaimed and put under cultivation.

By 1959, after expenditure of many billions of dollars, Gates (1968, p. 659) estimates that 30,738,115 acres of western lands had been irrigated, less than a third of Powell's optimistic estimate of 100 million acres appropriate for irrigation. It is difficult to evaluate the overall national return on this large investment in terms of either benefits or costs as they apply to irrigated lands. With respect to irrigation alone, it is undoubtedly true that many individual farmers and many regions have benefited greatly from the land reclamation program. Irrigation programs have been an important element in assisting the West to achieve growth rates considerably in advance of those of the rest of the nation. However, whether on net blance the nation has gained as much from the application of economic resources in irrigation of western lands as it might have from investment of these resources in other ways is questionable. Benefit estimates based upon subsidized prices for crops in surplus gave a distorted picture of return to society for investment in irrigation projects. Extensive evidence of waste, mismanagement and speculation were found in Congressional investigations of the programs in 1913 and again in 1924. Opportunities unquestionably exist for improving water management in the arid lands, but recent estimates by economists indicate that the benefit-cost ratios from utilizing scarce water in the West for municipal and industrial use could far exceed those from use in agriculture (see, for example, Wollman, 1962 and Young, 1969).

In the early years of the nation, the issue of retention of public lands versus disposal had been generally resolved in favor of complete disposal. By the end of the 19th century, most of the desirable agricultural land had been disposed of as well as much valuable timber, mineral, and grazing lands. When Frederick Jackson Turner (1894) announced the end of the frontier at the close of the century, he meant that the last free land suitable for agriculture under the Homestead Act had largely been taken up. However, as the frontier of free agricultural land disappeared and the nation became increasingly urbanized, heavily industrialized, and densely populated, sentiment gradually emerged for the retention of the remaining public lands. Along with increased awareness of the value to the nation of its public domain grew awareness of the need for improved practice in the management of land, air, water and other environmental resources, and in the operation of the public sector.

In response to growing dissatisfaction with the management of the Land Reclamation program, the Reclamation Bureau in more recent years has enlarged its program in cooperation with the Department of Agriculture, Corps of Engineers, Federal Power Commission and other agencies to embark upon extensive programs of providing water for hydroelectric power generation, flood control, water supply, navigation improvement, recreation facilities and a wide range of other activities. Congressional support for this enlargement of federal programs for regional development through development of natural resources was provided by the Taylor Grazing Act of 1934 which emphasized multiple-purpose planning of federal projects.

A basic assumption in multiple-purpose resource planning is that increased benefit-cost ratios can be achieved through combining projects which are complementary in order to achieve external economies and serve multiple objectives. Unfortunately, this principle has at times been misunderstood to imply that including more purposes in a project will automatically assure higher benefit-cost ratios, and has at times been used as a rationale for adding uneconomic projects (such as unnecessary dams) to programs (Behan, 1967).

The logic of multiple-purpose projects actually requires not maximization of the number of purposes to be served, but maximization of the overall benefit-cost ratio from the optimal combination of complementary purposes. Examples of purposes which might be complementary in a resource management project for public lands are reforestation, flood control, navigation, wild life management, and recreation. Grazing might be compatible with all of these uses, except forest management. Other uses which are usually preemptive of multiple-purpose management are mining, water impoundment, and intensive construction.

Recognition of the fact that some uses are preemptive and largely irreversible is giving rise to a better understanding of the role of the time-sequence and environmental change in natural resource management. For example, under certain conditions, the optimal multiple-purpose resource management plan may be to preclude inundation under a water impoundment, or to delay the use of land for development until minerals have been removed from below the surface. As regional development and economic activity become more intensive, awareness is increasing of the need for improved understanding of environmental management. One possible lesson to be learned from past efforts at U.S. programs of land management for regional development is the need for life-cycle planning and environmental responsibility so that on public or private lands uses are planned sequentially in order to do a minimum of irreversible damage and allow for future priorities in resource use. Market horizons and market prices are too biased towards the short run to indicate optimal long-run use of public lands, and in some cases private lands. This is one reason for recent programs to set aside public lands and resources for recreation, wilderness areas, and conservation programs (Krutilla, 1967).

Evaluation

In general, U.S. land grant and land management programs achieved their intended objectives. Despite inefficiencies and problems, it is estimated that 80 per cent of the public lands disposed of, outside of the South, ended up in single family farms. U.S. surveying procedures utilizing base lines and meridians helped identify boundaries and reduce uncertainty about titles. Disposal of western lands succeeded brilliantly in closing the frontier and in populating the West, which as a result experienced the fastest growth rates in the nation.

U.S. land policies were at least partially oriented towards achieving human objectives, rather than merely towards traditional aid to geographic regions and economic sectors. Primary concern was focused upon families of limited means, and there was recognition of need for investment in human capital of settlers, and concern for education. Provision was made for setting aside specified amounts of land in every area for the support of schools. This principle received its fullest recognition in the Morrill Act of 1862, which provided for the sale of public lands to establish land grant colleges, which revolutionized agricultural productivity and practice.

But despite its economic achievements, U.S. land grant policy may have had its greatest impact in terms of equity and social justice. John M. Brewster (1963) has noted that problems of class conflict, social tension, and distributive justice were eased in the U.S. by the deliberate policy of providing free land from the public domain to all who settled upon it. An urgent priority for society today is to find a twentieth century equivalent of free land. It is not clear in what direction the answer lies. However, given the nature of problems facing the poor in society today, it is probable that the answer lies in the direction of revolutionary improvements in education, health services, family planning, vocational training, income maintenance and welfare services. Programs of this kind oriented towards the cure of human problems may well be the contemporary equivalent of free land on the U.S. frontier.

Along with the impressive achievements of U.S. land policy in regional development should be noted what, by the advantage of hindsight, now appear to be mistakes, which should be avoided in the future regional development programs, and some possible suggestions for the future. As is noted in the section on internal improvements, it appears highly probable that the vast acreages given to promotors of railroads were far in excess of the amounts required to provide incentives and financial support for railroad construction. Serious errors were also made by treating land as homogeneous and by prolonged failure to classify and manage land according to its environmental characteristics such as climate, soil, topography, timber cover, mineral content, water supply, drainage, and other features. This failure led to problems for settlers, speculative excesses, losses to the public, and severe environmental damage. This problem was compounded by poor planning and administration of land programs. It is highly probable that a greater investment in public funds in staffing and administering land programs could have resulted in less speculation and abuses. However, it must be noted that in at least one early instance, namely land reclamation, in which the federal government did become deeply engaged in detailed planning, engineering, entrepreneurship, and administration, the early results left much to be desired.

One possible route for reasserting the importance of environmental management in the mainstream of U.S. practice is through the legal concept of waste. Marshall Harris (1963) has observed that in the successful U.S. efforts to free land use from restrictive European feudal rigidities, including the laws regarding waste of resources, we may have gone too far in the direction of freedom for land owners to pursue short-run profit objectives, and to treat resources as they please regardless of long-run irreversible damage to future generations. Although laws of waste still protect owners of land from damage by renters and others of 'lesser estate', the public interest might be better protected by a reexamination of application of some aspects of reasonable laws of waste to owners as well. As the earth becomes more crowded and more vulnerable to environmental damage from advanced technologies, there appears to be increasing merit in putting the burden of responsibility upon each decision maker, public, corporate and private to demonstrate responsible use of land, resources and environment in pursuing economic development and other goals.

CHAPTER V

River basin development*

Introduction

The management of its river basins has confronted the U.S. with the entire range of regional development issues explored in this study, but with particular emphasis upon problems of intergovernmental cooperation and conflicts between economic growth and environmental protection.

The history of river basin development in the U.S. is a testament to the belief that man's interests are served by conquering nature and that the application of engineering technology is a proper instrument for 'improving' natural river basins. In pursuit of these objectives, billions of dollars have been spent since the colonial period in the construction of canals, dams, levees, and other projects. Unfortunately, many of these projects have been undertaken for the achievement of short-run objectives, with inadequate understanding of the geology, hydrology, or ecology of the systems involved. And since river basins serve to drain large hinterlands, other economic activities have aggravated the problems of river basin management. Poor farming practices since the earliest colonial period led to rapid siltation of channels, flooding and silting up of seaports. Destruction of soil cover damaged the capacity of watersheds to absorb rainfall and release it to stream beds gradually, resulting in both aggravated flooding and low flows. Rather than correcting basic environmental causes, the remedy too often selected was to adopt an engineering approach to dredging channels and building levees.

These engineering works encouraged more settlement on flood plains, which increased the amount of human life and physical capital at risk,

* The author is indebted for assistance with this section to Professor Charles E. Olson of the Department of Business Administration and to Mr. Thomas E. Marchessault, and Mr. Craig Simmons of the Bureau of Business and Economic Research, all of the University of Maryland. Responsibility for the views expressed and for any errors, however, rests with the author.

thereby raising demands for more flood protection. Construction of additional levees only added to the severity of increased downstream flooding. Given the decreasing but finite probabilities of floods occurring over time beyond the containment capability of engineering works, low density development of flood plains with river basins left in their natural state has been recommended as an alternative to heavy investment in flood control programs.[1] Benefit-cost analysis would probably indicate some types of farming and other activities on flood-prone plains which would be economically justified even with periodic flood damage. This would be true where total costs, including costs of periodic recovery from flood damage, were exceeded by the benefits of a flood plain location over alternative locations. Full-cost insurance policies could be designed to spread the risk among flood plain occupants. However, it is questionable whether society as a whole should bear the cost of subsidizing flood plain development, especially when it compromises other environmental objectives.

The construction of dams has been widely justified in the U.S. partly as a mystical act of faith in the efficacy of huge engineering exercises, and partly on the basis of sophisticated analysis aimed at achievement of multi-purpose objectives. Among the benefits claimed for multi-purpose dams have been creation of water supply, irrigation, navigational benefits, prevention of siltation, electricity generation, flood prevention, low flow augmentation, dilution of pollution, and creation of recreational benefits. While all of these objectives are plausible, many scientists, environmentalists, and others are beginning to have serious doubts about man's ability to improve upon nature in the management of river basins.

Some of the problems which dams are intended to prevent are those created by or aggravated by other forms of human activity. These problems include siltation, pollution, and flooding. The eventual filling up of dams from siltation, natural and artificial, will leave a heritage of serious problems for future generations. The use of dilution as an anti-pollution measure is now recognized as an unacceptable substitute for prevention of pollution at its source. Most profitable irrigation projects were undertaken early by private investors, and many more recent federally subsidized irrigation projects have served to increase through crop subsidies the production of crops already in oversupply. A major problem with waterway improvements has been the impact upon the marine biology of fish and other species which through evolution over time adapted to natural river conditions and became dependent upon them. Most river basin engineering programs were undertaken with highly inadequate under-

1. See especially the work of Gilbert F. White, 1958, and Robert W. Kates, 1962.

standing of their ecological and environmental consequences. In the brief space available, a few examples of river basin management in the U.S. will be examined.

The Tennessee Valley Authority experiment

The Tennessee Valley is the best known U.S. venture in regional development. Its significance lies in the fact that a new agency was established, as in the case of so many U.S. efforts at regional development, which had a large measure of autonomy in its mission to deal with an entire system of rivers and tributaries.

The Tennessee Valley was, in 1929, an economically backward area. Per capita income in the area was forty-five percent of the national average with most of its population engaged in subsistence farming. The area was '... an agricultural region with few opportunities for industrial employment. Farms were small and farm families were large, so that many individuals who depended upon the land for a living were "underemployed". Aside from a large aluminum plant and a number of iron foundries, industry in the Valley was heavily concentrated in textiles and lumber, which paid low wages.'

The principle most closely associated with the TVA is the belief in man's right to use and reshape his environment to attain certain economic goals. This principle was applied to the extent that where the natural state of the Valley was not optimal for commercial and industrial activity, the TVA attempted reshaping the Valley.

According to the preamble to the enabling legislation, the purposes of the TVA were to:

> ... Improve the navigability and to provide for the flood control of the Tennessee River; to provide for reforestation and the proper use of marginal lands in the Tennessee Valley; to provide for the agricultural and industrial development of said Valley; to provide for the national defense by the creation of a corporation for the operation of Government properties at and near Muscle Shoals in the State of Alabama, and for other purposes (Clapp, 1955, pp. 55-56).

Navigation was originally considered as a peripheral objective of the Authority. Its importance was heightened, however, as the Authority ran into difficulties concerning its constitutionality. Prior to the TVA construction program navigation on the Tennessee River was limited. By 1930 numerous attempts had been made to open the River to traffic, but as an Army Corps of Engineer reported: 'The Tennessee River is not well adapted to navigation on a modern scale and completion of the existing projects would not provide a satisfactory waterway' (Droze, 1965, p. 17).

The original statute creating the TVA was unspecific about a navigation program for the Authority and its directors gave navigational programs only limited priority. This attitude was reversed for two reasons. The first was the wish of the Roosevelt administration to use the building of dams as a means of providing employment for the unemployed during the depression. The second was to minimize the chances of the Supreme Court declaring the entire project unconstitutional (Droze, 1965, pp. 21-22, 31-33).

Using a 1930 Corps of Engineers survey of the river as the basis for their blueprints, the Authority began immediate construction of a series of high dams. By 1945 the major portion of the construction had been completed and the shape of the Tennessee River had been altered substantially. The river had been transformed from a river with a 'year-round minimum of four feet upon forty percent of its course, two feet upon thirty percent of its course, and one and one-half feet upon the remaining thirty percent of its length' to one with a year-round minimum depth of nine feet for the whole length from Chattanooga to the Ohio River, a distance of six hundred twenty-seven miles (Droze, 1965, pp. 42-43, 62-64).

After construction of the waterway, it was necessary to construct terminal facilities if the river were to be used for freight transportation. The TVA then lent technical and legal assistance to groups that were attempting to persuade the various state legislatures to finance this construction. These groups were unable to convince the legislatures, however, and so the TVA decided to construct the facilities itself. They were built and operated by the TVA but were not used extensively until they were leased beginning in 1952 to private operators (Droze, 1965, pp. 72-79).

The dams built were high-water dams. For navigational purposes it made little difference whether the dams built were of this type or low-water dams. The low-water type, though cheaper and requiring less land, was ruled out because of uselessness for flood control. The high-water dams created massive reservoirs which stretched almost as far back as the next dam. After charting the rainfall and run-off cycles of the region the Authority was able to maintain reservoir depths so that during the wet season the reservoirs just fill without overflowing (Wiersena, 1955).

The Authority also compiles data on rainfall and run-off patterns in the Valley and conducts flood control studies for areas not directly adjacent to the reservoirs. These studies 'provide the basic information which the communities need to establish zoning and subdivision regulations to keep developments out of the flood plain... After a flood report is prepared, the TVA continues to assist the community in planning for flood damage preparation' (TVA, 1969a, p. 24).

Another element of the TVA project is its power program. At its inception the TVA acquired one hydroelectric plant at Wilson Dam and authorization to build others at various dam sites. The terms of the law allowed the TVA to sell surplus power to local communities, industry, the Federal government and private utility companies.

Most TVA power is sold to municipally-owned distributors and co-operatives who sell it to retail customers. The rates that these retail distributors may charge are closely controlled by resale agreements with the TVA.

Federal installations have become important customers of TVA especially since the construction of facilities in the area by the Atomic Energy Commission. In 1969 sales to the Federal government accounted for about seventeen percent of total sales. Power is also sold directly to about forty-three major industrial plants in the Valley. These sales account for about twenty-three percent of total sales (TVA, 1970, pp. 5-6, 38).

TVA power production originally came entirely from hydroelectric plants. By about 1950, however, there was little room for expansion of this type of plant, and TVA began construction of a series of coal-fired steam plants. In the mid-fifties the output from steam plants exceeded that from hydro plants. At present, steam plants account for over eighty-three percent of total power output. More recently the Authority has begun construction of nuclear-powered steam plants, the first of which was scheduled to begin operating in 1970 (TVA, 1970, p. 13).

The policy of the TVA with regard to rates has been that 'its electric rate should be as low possible to promote widespread, abundant use in the region' (TVA, 1970, p. 6). This policy of meeting all demand without raising rates has necessitated the expansion of power plants, resulting in a change in the primary source of energy from water power to coal. The increased emphasis on coal has made the TVA the nation's single largest consumer of coal. In order to keep coal costs down the Authority has tacitly approved the growth of strip-mining which is significantly cheaper than shaft-mining. Fifty percent of the purchases of coal by TVA are extracted by the strip method. The TVA has estimated that 25,000 acres of land have been stripped to get coal for their plants (TVA, 1963, pp. 5-6).

The TVA, arguing that their procurement policies are neutral with regards to strip-mining, point to their research in reclamation techniques and urge state and/or Federal control over the problem (TVA, 1963, pp. 8,12). The Chairman of the Board of Directors has argued the positive aspects of strip-mining: 'He asserted that the hundreds of miles of strip-mine haul roads and mountain cuts on the Kentucky landscape constituted a new resource in themselves, giving access for fire control and future recreational purposes. "Strip-mining, while it is going on, looks like the devil but what comes out of it has done wonders for this area. If you look at what those mountains were doing before this stripping, they were just growing trees that were not being harvested."' (*N.Y.T.*, 7-1-65, p. 33)

Opposition to strip-mining has grown and in 1965 the TVA agreed to include a proviso in its coal contracts for mandatory reclamation of stripped land. The effectiveness of this policy is not yet clear.

TVA has engaged in some positive conservation activities. These have included reclamation of eroded land and prevention of erosion. The TVA has done extensive work in planting trees and groundcover and in providing for drainage to avoid loss of topsoil.

In addition, in cooperation with the Bureau of Wildlife and Fisheries studies were undertaken to determine the effect of the reservoirs on animal and fish life. The major result of these studies has been the stabilization of reservoir levels during spawning seasons and the transferral to dry lands of food trees and shrubs which were flooded by the dams.

In recent years the TVA concept of conservation has been broadened to include the awareness of the need to maintain environmental quality. TVA has installed ash-collectors on the smoke stacks of coal-burning power plants, in order to decrease the amounts of solid wastes released into the air. It is also engaged in experiments with various methods of removing sulfur oxides from stack gases.

One area where the awareness of the danger of upsetting the ecological balance has resulted in a change of policy is in the area of flood control. In the past the TVA placed great emphasis upon building dams and levees to prevent flooding of inhabited areas. In recent years the thesis has gained increased acceptance that the banks of a river act as a natural flood control device and that human encroachment impairs this natural process. For this reason the TVA has urged that restrictions be placed on the development of flood plains (TVA, 1969b, pp. 25-26).

TVA is also making an effort to deal with thermal pollution from its nuclear and fossil fuel plants. A decision was made in 1965 to add a cooling tower to the Paradise Plant, which had been constructed in 1963 on a stream with relatively little cooling capacity. TVA has been criticized for failure to provide for cooling towers at its new Brown's Ferry nuclear power plant which is designed to permit water temperature outside the mixing zone in the stream to rise as much as 10°F. to a level as high as 93°F. The environmental effect of this temperature rise on the ecology of the stream is unknown, and while TVA has expressed concern and willingness to undertake research on the problem, it is following the usual practice of proceeding with construction first and performing the research after the fact. As in the rest of the nation, TVA continues to give economic development priority over environmental protection, though the balance may be changing slowly.

The economic impact of TVA is difficult to assess. Employment and real per capita incomes in the region have greatly increased since the program began, but analysts have been unable to determine how much better off, if any, the inhabitants are than if TVA had never existed (Moore, 1967). The availability of low-priced electricity, technical assistance, and other benefits of TVA has undoubtedly improved the lives of many who live in the region. On the other hand, no adequate yardstick exists for measuring the real loss to those who were moved away from their homes and farms in order to make way for the water impoundments. No adequate yeadsticks exist for measuring the ultimate ecological and environmental costs of converting a natural system of rivers into a managed, controlled system of waterways. A definitive study of the benefits and costs, and of who gained and who lost in the Tennessee Valley experiment, has yet to be made.

The Ohio River Basin

An excellent example of the heroic efforts needed to restore a river basin to health after it has been used primarily for waste discharge over a long period is the Ohio River story (see Cleary, 1967). Beginning at Pittsburgh and extending to Wheeling and Cincinnati through some of the most heavily populated and highly industrialized coal mining and steel producing centers in the U.S., the Ohio has become one of the most heavily polluted rivers in the nation.

The enormous task of dealing with this situation was undertaken by a new interstate agency, the Ohio River Valley Water Sanitation Compact (ORSANCO). Given the magnitude of the task, it is not surprising that the Ohio River remains one of the most polluted rivers in the U.S. despite the efforts of ORSANCO.

Beyond the sheer magnitude of the wastes discharged into the River, other serious problems of water management have plagued ORSANCO. One major problem has been that of obtaining agreement on objectives and division of costs between the many states, counties, and municipalities involved. The ORSANCO members have been frustrated by the fact that in some instances, after incurring heavy local costs to improve water quality, they have succeeded so well as to become ineligible for federal assistance under national programs later enacted, although the region is taxed like the rest of the nation to support these programs. Objectives of providing incentives and insuring equity would argue for some rectification of this situation to reduce the costs to pioneers in pollution abatement.

ORSANCO has succeeded in extending sewerage facilities to a large percentage of the total residents in its system. Its pioneering efforts have shown that regional organizations can evolve in response to local needs. However, very large problems still remain in abating pollution in the Ohio River and in restoring the River to health.

The Potomac River

The Potomac River is of interest not only as the river which flows through the nation's Capital, but as an example of the problems faced by a river which has remained largely unindustrialized. The Potomac is a particularly beautiful one, rising in the Appalachian mountains, running through the Piedmont Plateau to the fall line near Washington, and finally descending through the coastal plains as a tidewater estuary and tributary of the Chesapeake Bay.

The major problems of the Potomac result from pollution by pulp mills and acid mine drainage on the upper reaches, siltation over its entire range, and from massive metropolitan sewage discharges in the Washington area. Over many decades, the U.S. Army Corps of Engineers has proposed to construct an extensive series of high dams on the main stem and tributaries of the Potomac with the announced aims of preventing the occasional flooding of the Potomac, providing a water supply, and flushing pollution past Washington. In the 1950's, it was joined in these proposals by the Rural Electrification Administration which was interested in providing a public power supply for its member cooperatives, and a power cost yardstick in the region.

These plans were opposed by conservationists and others who preferred pollution reduction to pollution flushing, and who questioned the need for additional water supply and the feasibility of power production. As these objections emerged, the Corps of Engineers shifted the basis of its argument for high dams to rest largely upon the recreational benefits promised from the new lakes to be created. However, when it was pointed out that the dams would flood the C & O Canal and its foot paths which were already a favorite existing recreational facility, replace much of the natural flow with slack water, and create large mudflats from seasonal drawdowns of water from the lakes, much of the earlier support for the dams ebbed away. The Corps of Engineers continues to press its high dam proposals, but actual construction to date has been limited to a few branches off the main stem.

The tidewater reaches of the Potomac are notable for having supported for over three centuries a consistent and interrelated set of activities including agriculture seafood production, waterfowl propogation, recreation, and in more recent years, tourism attracted by historic restoration programs. Potential damage to these activities has recently emerged in proposals to construct industrial ports and oil refineries in areas of historic interest. A benefit-cost analysis of a proposed petroleum refinery indicated that expected benefits would be exceeded by losses suffered in the existing environmentally related activities if pollution and external diseconomies from petroleum refining reduced the growth rates of recreation, seafood production, and tourism (Dodge and Cumberland, 1970).

Evaluation

Management of the nation's river basins has offered a major testing ground for the hypothesis that through engineering practice, river basins can be modified to serve the ends of economic development. Redevelopment and use of waterways has contributed much to the wealth and affluence of the nation, and particularly in those regions having extensive river systems. However, recent concern over the long-range environmental damage inflicted upon river basins from waste discharge and physical modification has led to new efforts to understand river systems and to value them as irreplaceable national assets to regional development rather than as targets for exploitation. It is not clear that man has learned how to improve on nature in the design and management of large environmental systems such as river basins. In the long run, the most valuable asset in any regional development plan may well prove to be a natural unimproved river system.

CHAPTER VI

Urban development

As high density nodal regions, cities are the centers where society has both attained its highest achievements and generated its most critical problems. The central problem in city development is how to improve the quality of life in urban areas. Unfortunately, rapid economic growth in metropolitan areas and rising average incomes in the urban environment, where almost three-quarters of the U.S. population live, have failed to solve, and may indeed have aggravated, social problems. These problems include racial conflict, crime and violence, drug abuse, poverty, unemployment, mental and physical illness, housing deterioration, transportation breakdown, congestion, waste accumulation, environmental decay, and fiscal crisis.[1]

The U.S. value system has been ambivalent towards urban life from its earliest history. Jefferson deeply distrusted urban values, attributing many of the social problems he observed in eighteenth-century Europe to the influence of the city. He viewed the independent family farm as the source of civic virtue and social stability. However, there has always existed the opposing view of the emergence of the city as a precondition for specialization, diversity, culture, growth, affluence and progress.

But regardless of philosophical attitude towards urban life, city planners and developers have with little dissension viewed the business of the city as generating economic growth. Earlier chapters have suggested that from the beginning of the national period, regional economic policy in cities has emphasized competition for growth, particularly by overcoming spatial barriers through investment in transport systems. The most successful cities in this competition were those like New York, Baltimore, and Philadelphia which allocated their resources efficiently to provide a well planned transport system with profitable market and supply areas. In

1. For a more detailed examination of urban problems, see Perloff and Wingo Jr. (eds), 1968b.

the competitive race for urban growth, locational features and spatial relationships were critical, giving port cities at transportation breakpoints a particular advantage.[2] The availability of natural transport arteries, such as navigable or easily improved water routes, and absence of topographical barriers played a major role, as did efficiency, in planning the allocation of resources to improve and link up transport routes. Competition to be first in establishing linkages to the Great Lakes region and in being the first to breach the Appalachian barrier paid handsome dividends to New York and to Baltimore. This tradition was extended to urban competition for attraction of railroad routes, highways, and air routes.

The growth approach is firmly imbedded in urban economic development policy not only in the persistent effort to structure transportation systems for maximum local benefit, but also in intensive competition for the attraction of industry and other economic activity in order to utilize the transport and infrastructure facilities. The principle of urban competition for growth was established early and remains a central feature of U.S. urban economic policy in a period when its validity is much less obvious and when economic growth has become as much a problem as an answer to social problems.

While there have been losers as well as winners in the competition for urban growth in the U.S., and the fortunes of different centers have fluctuated over time, the net results of U.S. inter-urban growth competition have been successful in attracting sustained migration from rural areas into urban centers, in generating self-reinforcing economic development, and in achieving steadily increasing levels of per capita real income.

The urban population of the U.S. was only 5 percent of the total at the time of its first census in 1790, as compared to 95 percent rural, but by 1960, 70 percent was urban and only 30 percent was rural (Table A-5). Average per capita real incomes in urban areas, despite a high incidence of unemployment and poverty, are significantly higher than in rural nonfarm areas, and even higher than in rural farm areas.

Despite these impressive achievements in urban economic development in the U.S., while urban economic growth has succeeded in achieving its immediate objectives, that very success has aggravated other problems, generated a whole new set of problems, and has drastically changed the ordering of social priorities. Many of these new urban problems result from the inter-personal and inter-spatial distribution of the benefits and costs of urban growth. Just as the nature of earlier urban development

2. For an excellent treatment of the theoretical aspects of this phenomenon, see Hoover, 1948.

hinged upon urban-hinterland and inter-spatial linkages through transportation systems, current urban problems are dominated by the movements of disadvantaged displaced rural migrants into hostile urban cultures for which the migrants are unprepared. Under-employment or even unemployment with welfare payments are perceived to permit a better life in urban areas than in rural.

The counterflow of affluent commuters into suburban areas has been subsidized by federally financed highway systems and home loans, which lower the costs of living in the suburbs and of driving individual internal combustion vehicles back into urban job centers. External diseconomies to urban residents result from failure of commuters to bear the full social costs of pollution and congestion. While cities are faced with growing public sector costs to provide services and welfare for low income migrants, the major potential sources for tax revenue escape from the urban jurisdictions by moving into suburban areas.

Thus the urban areas, where social problems are most highly concentrated, are starved for tax revenue. Not only are programs for investing in human capital underfinanced, but the physical infrastructure of the urban core and its amenities are underfinanced, contributing to the physical decline of the urban environment. Because of concern that the benefits of local investment in human capital may 'spill out' of the region as educated, trained people migrate, local governments are unlikely to invest up to an optimal level in human capital programs. This is one of the major justifications for revenue sharing, from the federal to the state level, and from the state to the local level.

The tragic result of these forces is the concentration of the disadvantaged in urban centers which are unable or unwilling to provide the massive investment in human capital needed to improve the health, education, and productivity of ghetto dwellers. The highly visible contrast between the life style of the ghetto dweller and what he sees and expects from observation of the affluence around him results in frustration, alienation, crime, and violence. Unfortunately, the traditional appeal to competition for growth, attraction of industry and creation of jobs can not solve these urban problems as long as large numbers of urban dwellers have not been given the assistance needed to equip them to hold jobs and function productively.

The critical and chronic nature of urban problems in the ghetto tends to deflect attention away from other relationships between urban centers and their hinterlands. In addition to the traditional urban-hinterland linkages between market and supply areas and migration-commutation areas, urban areas have critical environmental linkages with their hinterlands, which have received inadequate attention in urban analysis. Urban areas draw their water supplies from water sheds which are usually far from the city limits. Similarly, they discharge sewage into rivers which spread the urban waste problem into downstream regions. Solid waste is customarily put into landfills in adjacent regions, or burned, creating an air pollution problem. In many ways urban areas provide positive external economies for their hinterlands in creating jobs and markets, but they also are the source of negative externalities in their expanding absorbtion of water and other environmental resources from their hinterlands and in their corresponding emission of liquid, gaseous, and solid wastes over growing areas. Clearly, a better understanding is needed not only of the economic linkages between urban areas and their hinterlands, but also of the environmental-ecological linkages involved.

One of the most graphic illustrations of the neglected interrelationships between megalopolis and the hinterland is the case of Los Angeles, which has often been identified as the early warning indicator of the future of urban problems.[3] An attractive climate, great natural beauty, the proximity of ocean beaches, deserts, and mountains all result in an environment which continues to attract millions to this rapidly growing metropolitan area. However, this very success in economic growth is a major threat to an area which extends much beyond Los Angeles to much of California. The requirements for water have been so great that the city of Los Angeles continues to extend its water supply system for hundreds of miles throughout California, so that there are few, if any, major waterways in the state which have not been impounded, relocated, redirected, straightened, lined with concrete, or confined within pipes. The magnitude of the sewage disposal problem is correspondingly great. The city's well-known smog problem was a precursor of what has become a general urban problem throughout the nation.

The technological system which contributed most to the growth of Los Angeles, the privately owned internal combustion automobile and highway, now constitutes a major problem for the city. Not only does it account for most of the smog problem, but early priority given to private autos and public highways destroyed the early public transportation systems and created the super-highways which dominate the city, its suburbs and the lives of its residents.

A wide range of programs and policies has been proposed for addressing the nation's urban problems. Among the most imaginative and controversial proposals have been those for creating new cities for the future. United States experience with new towns goes back to the Greenbelt towns of the 1930's, and the European experience with new towns has

3. For an excellent analysis of the development of Los Angeles, see Fogelson, 1967.

been followed with great interest. Recently interest has grown in proposals to construct large-scale, completely new urban centers designed to meet the needs of the future, and to design out as many social problems as possible. In some proposals, environmental quality would be achieved by total technological control, covering the entire area by a geodesic dome, within which air temperature, humidity, and climate would be completely controlled. This approach tends to write off the possibilities of protecting the total macroenvironment, in favor of creating small, controlled microenvironments (see Cumberland and Hibbs, 1970). Unfortunately, this approach would impose very heavy impacts upon the total external environment, because of its large requirements for power and waste disposal. The wave of the future may be suggested by the Houston Astrodome, already in use as a sports arena. But the replacement of its natural grass by artificial grass when it was discovered that the natural product would not grow under a glass dome and the problem of water run-off raise serious doubts among environmentalists.

A different set of proposals designed to save as much of the natural environment as possible is found in the imaginative plans of Paolo Soleri for his monumental, high-rise city machines designed to provide within one structure the housing, employment, and infrastructure needed for large population concentrations. Building up into the urban air space is substituted for urban sprawl and environmental destruction. Actually, almost self-sufficient urban structures for residence, employment, and recreation have been in existence for some time, though not on the scale envisaged by Soleri. However, it should be noted that these structures per se offer no solution to the environmental-ecological problem, outside their own microenvironments, from which they merely export waste problems.

In order to provide a viable approach to environmental-ecological problems, a new town or technological city would have to be based upon a total systems approach, far more advanced than those proposed to date. Ideally, all wastes would have to be internalized and recycled, so that harmful residuals, such as thermal waste from power production, could be used constructively for heating and cooling. This would have the double advantage of avoiding waste emissions to the environment and reducing the total amount of energy production. Planning an environmentally neutral new town would involve a level of technological, economic, environmental, and humanistic planning which is beyond the current state of the art. It would require a selection of types and scales of economic activities such that the residuals from each process could be constructively used by other processes.

Demanding though the technological requirements would be in designing an environmentally neutral city, they would be dwarfed by the economic, social and institutional requirements. Provision would have to be made for a rich variety of economic classes, skill levels, ethnic groups, and cultural types. The task of developing the enabling legal, fiscal and institutional arrangements would be formidable. The economic task of accumulating the vast amount of capital required, time phasing the construction, matching employment requirements with movements of persons with the necessary occupational skills, and providing linkages with existing facilities would be formidable. However, the challenge is one which should be met, at least experimentally in trial projects.

Harvey Perloff and his colleagues (1966) have emphasized that economic development is only one aspect of the more general phenomenon of urban and regional development. If the problems of lagging regions and deteriorating cities are to be understood and solved, they must be considered in terms of the institutional, governmental, legal and social interrelationships of development in general. The solution to urban problems can not wait for the design, testing, and construction of new cities. Perloff and others have urged the reconstruction of existing cities through the construction of 'new towns in town', in an effort to address the urban problems where they exist, and to provide jobs in the city where poverty and unemployment are concentrated. Other proposals, based upon the difficulty of creating new jobs in central cities, envisage suburban satellite concentrations as the appropriate location for new towns.

Moreover, the resolution of urban problems can not be achieved exclusively at the urban level. Urban problems are too closely linked to other national problems of population concentration, transportation, technology assessment, land use, fiscal federalism and related issues to be solved in isolation from these national issues. Improved management of urban problems will require national recognition of the relationships between these problems and development of coordinated policies and programs.

It will be necessary for the nation to decide over the long run on the extent to which it wishes to make life viable in rural and small town areas as compared with the present policy of implicitly encouraging rural migration into urban areas. Explicit spatial policies on optimal distribution of population as between rural, suburban, and urban locations is required. Difficult decisions must be made about large-scale technologies, such as transportation systems and the balance between public and private transportation. It will also be necessary for all levels of government, federal, state, and local, to coordinate fiscal and physical planning. More federal and state participation in physical planning will be essential to protect major environmental resources, such as water sheds, estuaries, and recreational resources, which have large spill-over effects among regions. Increased understanding of the linkages between urban concentrations and their hinterlands will be necessary to protect the quality of life and the quality of the environment. Following chapters will examine some possible elements of national policy on regional development, land use, and environmental management.

CHAPTER VII

The Area Redevelopment Administration

Introduction

In the field of national and regional economic development, goals, issues, and programs evolve over time as earlier goals are achieved and as exogenous factors change. As one set of problems is dealt with, the order of priorities changes. Federal land policy succeeded in settling the Western states and creating a highly productive agricultural base. Completion of the extensive systems of internal improvements provided the inter-regional transport network which linked the regions of the U.S. into a large efficient market and provided the basis for accelerated industrial development. Urban regions competed for growth, and special organizations evolved in order to manage the development of river basin regions.

Efficiency in production was encouraged by competition between economic activities as well as by competition between regions. Business and political leaders competed vigorously to establish their communities as termini for transport facilities and competed in other ways to increase their regional share of economic growth. As will be indicated in the section on the empirical results of regional development, these efforts were generally successful in achieving high average levels of economic development for the nation and in most of its regions. However, the very success of this regional economic development achievement by the middle of the twentieth century focused increasing attention upon those regions which had failed to share fully in the general prosperity of the nation. The contrast between the high national average level of affluence and the widespread pockets of poverty in rural areas, mountain areas, declining communities and urban ghettos became increasingly visible and increasingly challenging.

While earlier U.S. programs for regional development had been designed to accelerate local growth in particular regions and to bring all regions into the national market, a new concept was emerging of providing assistance to those regions which had failed to participate fully in the development of the national market, or which had actually suffered from the changing structure of the national market.

To an unusual degree, the development of national ideas and a national program for economic assistance to lagging regions resulted from the vision and efforts of one man. Paul Douglas, a distinguished former professor of economics and U.S. Senator from Illinois, began his efforts in Congress as early as 1955 to pass legislation to deal systematically with regional economic distress in the U.S. However, his early efforts were unsuccessful partly because of needs to clarify national goals in this new problem area, to debate the very complex and difficult issues involved, and to design programs which would be generally acceptable within the U.S. frame of values and purposes.

In May of 1961, largely as the result of years of effort by Senator Douglas, the U.S. embarked upon its first comprehensive program to promote economic development in all lagging areas of the nation. Legislation entitled the *Area Redevelopment Act* established the Area Redevelopment Administration (ARA) in the U.S. Department of Commerce (U.S. 1961). The basic issue of whether the use of public funds to aid lagging areas was justified was decided affirmatively. Also, the nature of the ARA program made it clear that while it was assumed that aid would somehow eventually reach needy individuals and families, the basis of expenditure was to be the region rather than individuals.

The basic idea of the ARA program was to make economic development assistance available to any eligible region which had persistent unemployment that exceeded the national average by a stated amount, or which had median incomes a stated percentage lower than the national median. The aid was in the form of technical assistance in planning, loans and grants for construction of public facilities, and low interest loans to private business firms.

Defining the region

Defining the types of regions eligible for aid was a critical issue for ARA. Recognizing the difficulties involved, Congress vested the ARA administrator with broad authority to define eligible regions, or areas as they were called in ARA parlance, and gave him latitude in determining the eligibility for aid.[1] The Act, however, did establish broad types of areas eligible for aid, designated by the section of the Act referring to them, as follows:

1. For further details on specific regulations and procedures of ARA, see Levitan, 1964.

Industrial areas (Section 5-a). These were identified as labor market areas as defined by the federal Bureau of Employment Security in cooperation with state employment services, usually having a labor force of at least 15,000, including 8,000 in non-agricultural employment. By January 1962, a total of 129 labor-market areas covering 240 counties had been designated as eligible for aid. An additional 657 counties, most of them having labor forces of less than 15,000, had been designated. Eligibility for aid in industrial areas was based upon a sliding scale of unemployment in excess of the national average, as follows:

1. unemployment averaging at least 6 percent for the 12 months preceding the application for aid, and in the qualifying period, and
2. unemployment at least 50 percent above the national average for one of the two preceding calendar years.

Rural and smaller urban areas (Section 5-b). These areas were defined in terms of counties in which farm families had low gross incomes and low levels of living. The level of living criterion was chosen rather than an unemployment criterion because the use of the latter criterion would miss large numbers of low income employed but underemployed persons who face poverty problems in rural areas. Eventually under this designation, ARA included 230 counties, which represented a complete list of counties the U.S. Department of Agriculture had intended to include under its proposed rural redevelopment program.

In some cases, special provisions were adopted to establish eligibility for counties which would not otherwise qualify by allowing counties or groups of counties contiguous to already designated assistance areas to be covered on the basis that they were part of an economic unit all of which had to be assisted in order to aid the most severely affected counties. Some 24 counties were included on this basis (Levitan, 1964, p. 63).

It was also found possible to qualify otherwise ineligible areas for aid by redrawing the officially defined boundaries of labor market areas, as was done in the case of several counties. Finally, Indian reservations were defined as economic areas eligible for aid. The labor markets designated included areas as small as counties, plus groups of counties, and some large metropolitan areas, such as Detroit and Pittsburgh. They were chosen on the basis of being chronic labor surplus areas. The 129 areas designated were in 29 states. Thus the issue of appropriate size and designation of the region eligible for aid was handled in highly pragmatic fashion. Congress left wide latitude to the discretion of the ARA administrator in defining eligible regions. The region was defined by the type of economic problem to be addressed.

The permissiveness of Congress in delegating aid guidelines to the ARA administrator and the traditional tendency in the U.S. to universalize programs geographically resulted in a very diffused pattern of eligibility. Within two years of beginning operations, ARA had designated as eligible for aid 1,061 separate areas, including approximately one-third of all of the counties in the U.S., with at least one county in every state and in American Samoa, Guam, the Virgin Islands, and Puerto Rico (Levitan, 1964, p. 66). The issue of concentration versus dispersion of aid had been unequivocally resolved in favor of dispersion. The question was how was the aid to be planned and administered.

Planning: The community overall economic development program

The authors of the Area Redevelopment Act had wisely included in it a provision that before an area could receive aid, it must submit a comprehensive community overall economic development program (OEDP).[2]

The intent behind this requirement for community planning and the specifications for it were farsighted and well designed. The plan was to be drawn up within the region by a broadly representative group of local citizens who were to specify the objectives and goals of the region to be achieved by the requested assistance. It was required that each investment under the program should assist the area in moving towards achievement of its goals. The OEDP was expected to analyze the regional obstacles to growth and to offer a plan for overcoming these obstacles in a manner consistent with a realistic appraisal of the area's comparative advantages and disadvantages.

Planning was recognized as a continuing process, which should involve all major community interests, such as business, labor, agriculture, and public officials. ARA was to provide guidance and technical assistance in preparing the OEDP's. Emphasis was put upon local involvement in order to identify local preferences about land use and zoning. Small areas were encouraged to coordinate plans for large-scale projects involving scale economies and externalities, such as transporation facilities, water resource development utility systems, manpower training, and resource development. Some counties were permitted to prepare combined OEDP's. In recognizing the need for regional planning based on more than one county, and in extending this principle to include areas involving more than one state, ARA made a particularly important contribution in launching regional planning efforts which eventually led to the separate multi-state Appalachian program.

If the quality of the OEDP's had met these specifications and if ARA

2. For details, see Dillon, 1964; and also Levitan, 1964.

had been able to evaluate the plans as visualized, the ARA performance could have been much improved. But in practice numerous problems occurred which impaired the value of the OEDP's. Funds were not provided to hire qualified experts to prepare the OEDP's. The ARA staff was too small to permit it to assist many of the local area planning groups, which as a result had to find local funds (often inadequate) for hiring staff, or had to rely upon the services of part-time and volunteer help of interested citizens. Even if ARA had offered funding for the purpose, there were not enough qualified experts in regional economic planning to do an adequate job for all of the areas involved. In many cases in which local funds were provided for the purpose, the OEDP's were prepared by groups oriented towards engineering, physical design or other interests which did not necessarily qualify them to deal with regional economic development problems.

Despite requirements for broad community representation, the local planning efforts often tended to be heavily influenced by the local financial, business, and construction groups who dominated the local economy and who had much to gain from regional development as conventionally conceived. One reason for the dominance of OEDP planning by the business community was the fact that the local Redevelopment Area Organizations required by ARA and expected to provide broad community representation were often formed simply from existing local business development groups. Consequently, the resulting OEDP's reflected their interests in attracting industry, aiding real estate developments, acquiring plant sites, constructing new plants, and providing financial assistance to new or expanding firms (Levitan, 1964, pp. 195-200).

This orientation towards progress through pouring of concrete was encouraged by the traditional U.S. view of regional development and was reinforced by the concept of regional development as viewed under the Area Redevelopment Act, which was essentially physical construction of public and private facilities, rather than broad general regional development. Consequently, it should not be surprising that many OEDP's turned out to be shopping lists of separate projects for 'earth moving' (Levitan, 1964, p. 219) favored by the business community, rather than long-run plans for improving the quality of life in the region.

The quality of the data and analysis in many of the OEDP's was poor and rarely were efforts made to estimate the benefit-cost ratios of alternative approaches to regional development. Heavy reliance was placed upon attracting new manufacturing plants into the region at a time when manufacturing employment was growing slowly in the nation. As the result of strong opposition in Congress, pirating firms from one area to another by the use of local subsidies was not permitted, but even this issue was compromised by permitting attraction of new branch plants from firms with plants in other regions. In practice, the ARA resisted giving aid to areas which used local subsidies to attract industry.

Problems of the substantive quality of the OEDP's were compounded in Washington by the limitations of staff and budget for evaluating and processing the deluge of these plans. Facilities both for providing technical assistance in the field and for administration in Washington were inadequate for the purpose. Continued pressures from local areas and from their Congressional representatives resulted in *pro forma* approval of many proposals before they could be given adequate review or revision. Consequently, much of the useful intent behind the idea of the OEDP was never realized. The failure to generate good local plans necessarily limited the nature of the results which could be expected from the already limited range of loans and grants programs provided for under ARA.

ARA commercial and industrial loans

A basic assumption behind the ARA legislation had been the need for special credit facilities for chronically depressed areas because conventional lenders were not sufficiently venturesome, or had exhausted their legal lending capacity, or because of other imperfections in the capital market. Therefore making low interest loans to firms locating or expanding in depressed areas was a major component of the ARA program. Little opposition was encountered to this program, for numerous reasons. Federal credit facilities had traditionally been used for development purposes. In this case, ARA gained the support of the banking establishment by permitting them to participate in loans and by giving repayment to banks precedence over repayment to the federal government. ARA loans could amount to as much as 65 percent of the total cost of land, buildings, equipment, and machinery, but funds could not be loaned for working capital. Rather than process loans itself, ARA chose the Small Business Administration (SBA) as the agency designated to evaluate proposals with final determination by the ARA administrator. The SBA was also permitted to participate in making loans for area redevelopment purposes.

The Act required that the local area participate in the financing of projects to the extent of providing 10 percent of the loan or the equivalent in land and buildings in an effort to assure some minimal evidence of the soundness of projects. Repayment could extend over 25 years. At the insistence of Congressmen from already industrialized areas, the bill prohibited loans to establishments moving from one area to another, although many southern legislators favored the idea of relocation.

Applicants were also required to demonstrate that they had applied for loans first through commercial credit facilities, and that credit was not available from them. Some states assisted local areas in providing the non-federal share.

ARA had to face the fact that low interest loans to some firms could cause problems to competitors in the same industry. Although this is not necessarily undesirable from the viewpoint of the national economy, it became ARA policy to exercise caution in using public tax revenues for granting loans which might cause competitive problems for other firms.

Aside from these permissive guidelines, Congress imposed virtually no limitation upon the administrator's freedom to grant loans. Under the pressure of events, ARA itself was unable to develop effective guidelines. By 1963, ARA had approved 168 loans for a total of more than $51 million. The average size of loans was about $330,000. Loans were made primarily for manufacturing activities, with the largest amounts going to lumber and wood products and food processing. The largest loans to non-manufacturing activities were in the field of recreation and tourism.

In order to be able to achieve a high ratio of jobs created to expenditures incurred, the agency preferred to make loans in industries having a low amount of investment required per worker. However, ARA was willing to depart from this rule of thumb under some conditions, especially where large local employment multipliers could be expected. This rationale was used to justify loans made in some areas for highly criticized recreational complexes. There is no *a priori* reason why recreation and tourism cannot contribute as positively to regional development as can industry. In fact, these activites are growing faster than manufacturing in the U.S., and may offer regional development advantages over some types of manufacturing activities, especially of the pollution-intensive variety, despite the fact that they are seasonal, and pay low wages.

ARA loans and grants for public facilities

The Area Redevelopment Act included provisions which recognized that the health of regional economies depends upon successful functioning of the public sector as well as of the private sector. It therefore provided funds for making loans and grants to improve the infrastructure of local communities.

The terms of eligibility for public facilities required that they conform with the economic development program of the community, that the funds must not be available on reasonable terms elsewhere, and that the project must improve the opportunities for establishment or expansion of industrial or commercial plants (Levitan, 1964, p. 136). The argument is often made on behalf of industrial development that it is a necessary step in order to provide tax revenue for the improvement of public services. The ARA requirement for public facility loans that they must tend to improve the opportunities for industrial or commercial development indicates a reverse order of priorities.

By May of 1963, ARA had approved 92 applications for public facility projects for a total of more than $46 million. Of these, 79 were for development of industrial parks, utilities, water supplies, sewerage systems, and port facilities and the rest were for recreational facilities and research projects (Levitan, 1964, p. 146). As in the case of ARA loans for private recreational facilities, use of public funds for public recreation facilities generated opposition.

Before ARA had developed its own modest public works program, it was given authority to administer a much larger public facilities program under the Public Works Acceleration Act of 1962. Because improvement in the overall level of national economic recovery still left pockets of unemployment, which tended to confirm the structural unemployment hypothesis, this act was adopted as an emergency measure to provide immediate employment. The new program was also justified on the basis that the original ARA program was designed as a continuing effort to aid communities in solving their long-run problems of chronic unemployment.

The new program provided a total of $850 million for accelerated expenditures on public works through June 1964. Eligibility requirements provided that expenditures generate immediate useful work, meet essential public needs, and be consistent with locally approved comprehensive development plans. Guidelines were minimal but wide geographic distribution was strongly suggested. ARA worked with other agencies which it designated to manage specified programs. Grants for hospitals, health facilities and sewage treatment plants were handled by the U.S. Department of Health, Education, and Welfare. Agencies designated for administration of other types of accelerated public works were the U.S. Departments of Interior, Commerce, Army Corps of Engineers, General Services Administration, Post Office, TVA, Coast Guard, and Veterans Administration. The funds were used primarily for public utilities, roads, waste treatment plants, hospitals, public buildings, and recreational facilities.

Manpower training

Most of the funds expended by ARA for the purpose of alleviating regional economic distress were disbursed in the form of loans to business and loans and grants for construction of public facilities on the assumption that assistance to business and public facilities would eventually create jobs and income for the poor and the unemployed. Only a very small fraction of the total ARA funds was spent directly in the form of aid to individuals. These were funds used to finance a modest job training program.

Rapid technological change in the U.S. economy made the experience and skills of much of the labor force obsolete and generated the need for continuous upgrading of labor force productivity. The problem was particularly acute in distressed areas. Senator Douglas and others recognized that construction of factories and providing job opportunities in these areas was unlikely to result in actual employment unless workers could be given the skills required for the jobs.

In administering its vocational training program ARA operated through existing agencies with related responsibilities. The U.S. Department of Labor determined training needs. The Department of Health, Education, and Welfare determined the course content and contracted with state authorities to administer the training. The U.S. Department of Agriculture advised on training in rural areas, as did the Bureau of Indian Affairs on programs for Indian reservations.

By 1963, applications had been approved to train more than 19,000 persons in 386 separate projects at a cost of almost $11 million, for an average cost per trainee of $567 (Levitan, 1964, pp. 176-177). Training was provided in 170 occupations, including machine-tool operation, typing, stenography, sewing machine operation, and welding. New courses were organized for maintenance and repair of farm machinery, and electronics assembly.

The ARA training efforts were among the most promising and fruitful parts of the total program. Experience gained emphasized the needs and opportunities for coordinating what had previously remained independent programs of employment services and labor market information, guidance and counseling, vocational education, on the job training, and estimation of manpower requirements. The experience gained in these areas under ARA contributed to the establishment of a much larger manpower program, the Manpower Development and Training Act, which once more followed the tradition of extending services orginally designed for those areas which were most distressed, to all regions of the U.S.

Evaluation

The Area Redevelopment Administration from 1961 to 1965 provided the U.S. with its first experience from a program designed to offer assistance on a comprehensive basis to all regions where levels of income and employment lagged below certain levels. While ARA did not succeed in solving regional development problems in the U.S., it did achieve what it was directed to do by Congress, and contributed valuable experience which served as the basis for an improved program which succeeded it, the Public Works and Economic Development Act of 1965 (EDA).

The objectives of ARA were to reduce unemployment and increase incomes in areas of chronic economic distress. During the period of its operation, employment did increase and incomes did rise in many areas where ARA projects were undertaken. However, it is very difficult to estimate how much of this improvement should be directly attributed to ARA activities. Some of this improvement would have occurred without ARA assistance. It is difficult to determine how much activity in ARA areas might have otherwise occurred in other regions. Furthermore, it is impossible to determine what would have been the pattern of development without any ARA program, just as it is impossible to determine what would have been the impact of alternative programs, such as those putting more emphasis upon direct aid to individuals for raising productivity. A major problem in the concept of ARA was its heavy emphasis upon aiding regions rather than aiding individuals. There is very little theoretical or empirical evidence to justify the overwhelming emphasis that ARA placed upon channeling aid expenditures to the public and private sectors within distressed regions rather than addressing directly the productivity and other problems of the low income and unemployed persons in these regions. It would have been valuable to have experimented with more programs like the small manpower training program as alternatives to the business loans and public works programs. ARA programs were dominated by the traditional and conventional U.S. concept that aid to individuals could best be justified if it were channeled through the market in the form of aid to businesses and through the public sector primarily in the form of earth moving, concrete pouring and construction of physical facilities.

A major obstacle to the analysis and improvement of ARA programs was the neglect of research in the overall effort. For an expenditure of a very small percent of its total budget, ARA could have explored methods to improve its statistical base, evaluate program effectiveness, examine alternative programs, and to develop improved guidelines for making loans and grants. The failure to develop a strong research capability within ARA and with academic and other independent research groups was a critical error which aggravated all other ARA difficulties.

The inability to develop effective guidelines and priorities within ARA limited the ability of the agency to turn down questionable proposals, or to resist political pressures, and led to uncoordinated and diverse spreading of funds. More concentration of aid in areas where lasting results could have been achieved would have been preferable. The effort to please everyone and help every region resulted in spreading aid too thinly. A much higher level of selectivity for regions and for projects could have improved the quality of ARA performance. The ARA basic concept of regional development was an excessively narrow one which depended heavily upon achieving development goals through efforts to act upon regional markets by channeling expenditures through public facilities and private business firms.

As Senator Douglas often observed during his pioneering efforts to gain acceptance for the idea of a regional development program in the U.S., ARA did not promise to accomplish everything, but it was a beginning. The ARA program did result in valuable contributions. A most important achievement was to require that objectives for regional development be spelled out by local development advisory groups having broad community representation. Unfortunately in practice representation often did not extend beyond narrowly oriented business groups, and ARA was unable to offer imaginative leadership and guidance in identifying community goals. However, the concept of the community overall economic development program is a valid one.

ARA demonstrated a flexible pragmatism in defining regions, in establishing eligibility criteria, and in attempting to coordinate the interests of all levels of government and all agencies with related programs. The resulting consensus-based approach caused almost all issues to be blurred and compromised rather than to be faced and resolved. However, this may have been a justifiable price to pay for gaining acceptance of the program. The pluralistic, permissive approach to settlement of issues and conflict resolution had become hallowed in earlier U.S. experience in regional development. The beginning made by ARA provided the basis for an improved program under the successor agency, the Economic Development Administration.

CHAPTER VIII

The Economic Development Administration

Introduction

The Area Redevelopment Administration, in establishing the legitimacy of comprehensive regional aid, had demonstrated that new programs of channeling public funds into regions of chronic underemployment and low incomes could not only gain acceptance within the U.S. political framework, but that this kind of program yielded net political benefits as well as possible net economic benefits. Logical next steps were then to expand the program, correct some of its deficiencies, and extend it to more areas. These were the objectives of the Public Works and Economic Development Act of 1965 (Public Law 89-136. See U.S., 1969).

The program

The Economic Development Administration (EDA) was an evolutionary variation of its predecessor Area Redevelopment Administration (ARA) which attempted to correct some of the more obvious faults of the earlier efforts but without innovating to a degree which would generate public and congressional opposition.

The EDA program consisted of:

		Annual Authorization (in millions $)
Title I	Grants for Public Works and Development Facilities	500
Title II	Other Technical Assistance	170
	A. Loans for public works and development facilities	
	B. Guarantees of working capital loans	

Title III	Technical Assistance, Research, and Information	25
	A. Technical assistance studies in areas needing assistance	
	B. Grants to planning and administrative organizations	
	C. Research program	
	D. Independent study board to investigate the effects of government procurement and other programs on economic development	
Title IV	Establishment of Area and District Eligibility	50
	A. Redevelopment areas, based upon levels of unemployment and low family incomes (with at least one in every state)	
	B. Multicounty economic development districts containing two or more redevelopment areas and at least one development center	
Title V	Regional Action Planning Commission	15
	A. Multistate economic development regions	
	B. Regional commissions to administer development regions	
Title VI	Administration	
	A. Administration by administrator under the Secretary of Commerce in consultation with other agencies	
	B. Establishment of a National Public Advisory Committee on Regional Economic Development	
Title VII	Technical and Administrative Provisions	
	A. Prohibits assistance to projects in industries which have excess efficient capacity	
	B. Authorizes use of facilities and services of other agencies	
	C. Extends benefits from ARA to redevelopment areas under EDA	
Total, all programs		760

In its operations, EDA carried on very much in the same pattern as did ARA. The primary legal criteria in determining the eligiblity of an area for aid under EDA regulations were that the area, which was usually a county, have an unemployment rate greater than 6 percent or a median family income of 50 percent of the national median or less. Areas not meeting these tests might qualify under other secondary tests.

The failure of ARA to undertake a research program capable of reviewing goals, of clarifying issues in regional development and of advancing the understanding of the theoretical problems involved left EDA little option but to deal initially with the issues very much as did ARA. Many ARA programs were carried forward under EDA, with the same staff.

EDA based its program upon the assumption that regional adjustment could improve national economic performance and rejected the idea of accepting market results as optimal spatial patterns of economic activity. On the issue of place prosperity versus people prosperity, EDA came down even more heavily than ARA in opting for aid to places. However, it is important to note that some manpower programs and other programs designed to deal directly with the productivity and other problems of persons were established in EDA and in other agencies. However, EDA clearly gave priority to regional economic development rather than to general regional development or to alleviation of poverty.

The issue of migration was regarded by EDA very much as it had been under ARA, as a phenomenon to be explicitly avoided. EDA did not embark upon large-scale efforts to aid persons to migrate from one area to another. Nor could EDA loans be used to relocate jobs, especially in 'highly mobile, intensely competitive industries, such as the apparel or garment industry, in which substantial unemployment and unused capacity exists' (U.S., 1969b, p. 10).

Although EDA initiated research on the problem of equity versus efficiency, it continued to pursue both objectives, adopting a 'worst first' policy for welfare purposes, as well as looking for projects with high potential payoffs in pursuit of the efficiency objective. However, the nature of the conflicts between these objectives was explicitly faced under EDA.

Unlike ARA, EDA did not exclude urban ghettos from eligibility for assistance. However, during its early period, few entire cities met the low income and high unemployment criteria needed to qualify for aid, and by law, individual separate parts of cities were not permitted to qualify. Therefore, EDA, by necessity, left the problem of urban assistance essentially to the U.S. Department of Housing and Urban Development, the anti-poverty program, and other programs oriented towards the urban poverty problem. There were other significant changes from ARA orientation and operations under EDA. One of the most important corrective efforts of EDA was to develop within a short period a comprehensive research program. EDA management recognized that in addition to having close research linkages with the academic community, it needed strong research capabilities within its own organization. A complementary relationship is needed between internal and external research because of the different objectives and comparative advantages of the two groups. In the social sciences, universities have a comparative advantage in basic theoretical speculative research intended to advance the state of knowledge. Academic research, as a result, often appears to be theoretical and unresponsive to the current operating needs and policy decision problems of government agencies. It is difficult for government agencies to insure the relevance of government sponsored academic research to what agencies conceive to be their high priority policy problems without appearing to infringe upon the self-direction and freedom of the academic researcher. Government agencies therefore attempt to conduct their own research in the hope that it will be more relevant and more sharply focused upon their problems as they see them. However, the unremitting pressures of continuous high priority operating problems make it difficult for qualified researchers in government to find the insulation from short-run distractions and the protection against administrative demands upon their time so that they can devote sustained effort to long-range research.

These issues are difficult to resolve, but an effective approach followed by EDA was to recruit a distinguished inhouse research group partly from universities which, by means of its close relationships with academicians, attempted to contract for external research which would be both academically significant and also relevant to regional economic development policy and operating problems. One result from the EDA research program has been the output of many research papers both within the agency and in professional journals which have identified and sharpened conceptual problems in the field of regional development.[1]

The EDA approach to the issue of defining regions differed from that of ARA. Dissatisfaction with the lack of guidelines for geographic allocation of aid under ARA, and the hope of achieving better regional development results from concentrating aid in critical amounts for sustained development led to legislative provision in EDA for identifying multicounty economic development districts containing two or more redevelopment areas with at least one development center. The provision for aiding development centers in Title IV of the EDA legislation represents legislative acceptance of the concept of growth poles which developed largely from the work of the French economists Perroux, Boudeville, and Lajugie (Hansen, 1968, chap. 5). The theoretical justification for the growth center concept is that while indiscriminate dispersal of necessarily limited funds for regional development on a fair shares basis

1. See the U.S. Department of Commerce, Economic Development Administration series, *The Research Review*, for status reports on this research program and for summaries of research projects.

is likely to result only in a costly, ineffective effort to resist market forces, concentration of this aid at a limited number of viable locations is more likely to result in self-sustained growth because of achievement of economies of scale and generation of external economies.

In addition to having advantages in theory, adoption by EDA of the growth center concept was helpful in meeting operating problems. Emphasis upon growth centers rather than fair shares to all regions offered a guideline in allocating scarce resources and provided some protection against political pressures for questionable projects. Assistance to a limited number of growth centers also offers an approach to the migration dilemma by offering what have been termed countervailing targets for short-range local migration, as alternatives to migration out of congressional districts (Cameron, 1969b).

The emerging literature on growth points represents an important advance in approaching the difficult but basic issue of explicit analysis of spatial relationships between activities in regional development. EDA has taken another important step in that direction by addressing the more general problem of city size distribution. The problem of moving from consideration of historic and current city-size distribution and location towards identification of probable and preferred future patterns is an extremely difficult one. It involves problems of different densities of economic activity per unit of space, economies of scale in the provision of public services, trends in migration patterns and many other difficult issues. However, it will be impossible to develop an overall strategy for regional development in the U.S. until benefits and costs can be identified for alternative patterns of city size and location. EDA has begun to address this problem by undertaking research on changing industrial location patterns and migration (McGuire and Harris, (b)).

Growth point strategy raises other difficult issues in regional development. Conversion of a non-growth center into a successful growth center may require a costly combination of factors, not all of which can be determined in advance. Those centers having the highest probability of success are likely to be ones which are already demonstrating the capability for growth, raising again the equity versus efficiency argument. In addition, the requirement of designating growth centers involves an explicit and politically sensitive decision on what areas are to grow and what areas are not. However, explicit acceptance of responsibility to designate growth-no growth areas is ultimately required by the logic of a national policy on regional development.

Evaluation

EDA, like ARA, has attempted to deal with the problem of geographic concentration of poverty and unemployment by providing aid to public and private sector activities in depressed regions. A major program in each agency has been that of providing loan capital subsidies to existing and new businesses. A special survey of firms assisted by ARA concluded that loans totaling $7,607,000 resulted in creation of 951 jobs at a cost of $8,000 per job, or creation of about 12.5 jobs for each $100,000 loaned (Gaskins *et al.*, 1968). Similar analyses of firms assisted by EDA suggested somewhat improved performance, with the loan cost of jobs ranging from $5,431 to $7,463, or jobs created per $100,000 of loans amounting to from 13.4 to 18.9.

However, the loan cost per job does not represent true cost to society because part of the total money loaned will be repaid. In order to obtain a better indicator of the cost to the nation per job created by ARA and EDA loans, the authors made allowances for loan repayments and losses, administrative costs incurred, and alternative interest earnings which might have been received if the funds had been loaned instead in the private sector at a 10 percent interest rate. Depending upon alternative assumptions about the loss rate on loans, the study estimates the measurable costs to society per job created by the ARA-EDA loans of from $1,384 to $4,377 (Gaskin *et al.*, 1968, p. 7).

The study also makes estimates of the amount of income generated per job from ARA-EDA loans under various assumptions. Assuming an income multiplier of 1.2, and average annual income per job of $5,568, each ARA-EDA generated job produced total incomes of $6,682 (or $8,352 with a 1.5 income multiplier). Benefit-cost ratios of greater than one were derived, indicating a favorable return to society from the ARA-EDA business loan programs.

The authors note that limitations on the reliability of these results could modify the interpretation of the results. The study ignores the amount of complementary funds provided by state, local, and private sources. Causality can not be demonstrated in this kind of analysis. Some of the jobs created may have reduced the number of other potential jobs elsewhere.

Together, ARA and EDA have made loans of about $250 million with losses to date of about $15 million, in creating an estimated 20,000 jobs. However, no adequate long-run benefit-cost analyses have been made under ARA or EDA of the comparative advantages of creating jobs through subsidies to business as compared with creating jobs through upgrading skills, raising individual productivity, and through other programs focused upon the needy individual rather than upon the business enterprise. The existence of a multi-million dollar program under pressure to get things done to aid business in distressed areas constitutes an incentive to the promotional lobbyist with political connections who becomes adept at designing projects to meet the loan requirements, then leaving with his commissions, fees, and profits whether the project has long-run viability or not. If the operation is a marginal one, the federal agency may be tempted to pump in additional increments of aid in order to avoid failures and publicity adverse to the program.

In seeking to aid the poor through largesse to business, other serious difficulties arise. The administrator must make choices between competing firms and proposals that are influenced by political pressures as well as by pure market efficiency, and political favoritism is difficult to avoid when an agency's congressional appropriation may be in jeopardy. It is difficult to arrive at the proper distinction between legitimate congressional action on behalf of constituents and improper conflict of interest.

Efforts to aid the needy through subsidies to capital under both ARA and EDA have encountered an inherent problem. If the financial incentives and subsidies were large as they would need to be to influence the locational decisions of large, successful firms, much of the federal funds would be allocated to already affluent businesses. But on the other hand, if the financial incentives were kept at a modest or inadequate level, the program would tend to attract marginal firms with a high probability of eventual failure which would result in downward multiplier effects.

The concept of regional development adopted by EDA and largely taken over from ARA was an extremely limited one, emphasizing economic development (rather than general regional development or rather than alleviation of poverty) insofar as it could be achieved through loans and grants to public agencies and private business. Despite good intentions, the inadequacy of staff and resources available for local planning prevented formulation of regional plans which specified broadly based community objectives. Resources were also inadequate to support benefit-cost analyses of alternative programs for achieving the objectives. Despite a new emphasis upon concentrating aid in growth centers, the research resources necessary to assign growth center priorities, identify their hinterlands, and measure the linkages between them were inadequate.

The provision for establishing at least one redevelopment area in every state regardless of qualification or need is an excellent example of the tendency towards unselective proliferation of U.S. development programs. It violates both equity and efficiency standards, but may be defended on the basis that such concessions are a necessary price of admission for the acceptance and testing of new programs.

Both ARA and EDA, in their efforts to provide economic assistance to people in distressed areas, have accepted the strategy of working through the operation of the market place while making marginal adjustments in the locational outcome of market decisions. This is a strategy which has both compelling advantages and serious problems. A major attraction of the market approach is that it is hallowed by U.S. tradition and historical precedent. Ideally, incremental amounts of federal subsidy in loans or guarantees can activate large investments of private capital, yielding a high benefit-cost ratio for successful projects. If all goes well, federal manipulation of the market economy can also keep governmental responsibility for administration to a minimum.

However, serious problems must be recognized in adopting a federal strategy of aid to distressed areas through aiding private business. First there is the problem that much of the money involved will accrue to influential, affluent promoters rather than to the purported clientele of the needy, the unemployed, and the underemployed. Even if the project is successful and jobs are created, the firm will be inclined, under competitive pressures, to hire the most productive labor possible per dollar of expenditure. It may therefore bring in skilled labor from outside the distressed region rather than hire the local unemployed, particularly if their productivity is low, as it is likely to be in chronically depressed areas.

In appraising the strategy of aiding individuals through attempts to cause readjustments in market place decisions, it is instructive to reconsider early U.S. regional development efforts through disposal of the public lands. The initial efforts to get land into the hands of bona fide settlers by manipulating the land market through variations in the price of public lands, length of loan requirements, interest rates, use of military script, all tended to enrich the land speculator and exclude the small holder. Not until the Homestead Act of 1862 was this situation corrected by straight-forward action tailored objectively by outrights gifts of land to those willing to settle upon it. In its regional development programs, the U.S. has yet to design the contemporary equivalent of the Homestead Act.

CHAPTER IX

The Appalachian Regional Commission

Introduction

While EDA was based upon ARA and represented an evolutionary departure from its predecessor agency, the Appalachian program emerged from ARA activities in a very different format. By spring of 1960, the nation's attention had become focused upon Appalachia by several developments. The presidential primary elections in West Virginia had given the candidates a first-hand look at the severe economic hardships in the area and television coverage of the campaign gave millions of Americans a first close look at the implications of large-scale chronic regional distress. The candidates competed in promising regional aid programs. On May 8, 1960, the governor of Maryland convened a group of Appalachian governors to design a program for aid to the entire region. By the following year, a program was presented by the governors to President Kennedy who directed ARA to assist the governors in developing their program. After years of study and consideration, which were continued by the next administration, President Johnson proposed legislation to the Congress, which on March 9, 1965, passed the Appalachian Regional Development Act (Public Law 89-4).

Objectives

In comparison with the harshness and severity of the poverty in Appalachia, the statements of objectives in the official documents and reports of the Appalachian Regional Commission have been understated and modest (ARC, 1968, p. 13). The fundamental objectives of the Appalachian program are to help the people of the region to overcome the problems that face them, to reverse the damages which have been done to the people and the resources of the region, and to improve the quality of life for the residents of Appalachia.

The problems in Appalachia are complex, and of long standing. It was noted earlier that under colonial development policy, settlers were vigorously discouraged from moving westward because of British concern for monopolizing the fur trade and avoiding conflict with the Indians. Settlers who defied this policy sought out isolated locations at the heads of mountain hollows in order to elude both the Indians and the militia. From the beginning, they suffered from the penalties of marginal locations and cultural isolation. However for almost a century, the Appalachian settlers maintained a self-sufficient culture based upon agriculture, hunting and handicrafts that was in approximate equilibrium, though at a low level of economic activity, with their environment.

Economic and social disaster began for the people of Appalachia when the outside world, under pressures of the industrial revolution, discovered the value of natural resources in the region, and began to exploit them as absentee owners. The virgin forests were the first resource to go. Timber rights were acquired over vast tracts by representatives of timber companies at very low prices.[1] Short run profit objectives and competitive pressures led to mining of the timber using destructive practices which stripped away the soil cover on steep slopes. Consequently, not only was the timber lost without regard to reforestation, but the soil from the slopes was left to wash down into the streams. The timber companies found it cheaper to purchase timber rights, cut the timber, and move on, letting the land erode, rather than acquiring the land, paying taxes, and reforesting.

The next wave of destruction was created by strip mining the rich coal reserves of Appalachia. In this case also, absentee coal companies acquired mineral rights at low cost from mountain people who were ill prepared to protect their rights or interests. The leases gave the miners unqualified rights to do whatever was necessary to remove the coal. Bulldozing the sides of mountains to get at the coal created spoil banks which slid down upon mountain farms and houses, destroying everything in their path and blocking waterways. The land owners were powerless to protect their land or their homes (see, for example, U.S. 1968b).

Water runoff from mined areas was contaminated by sulphur and other elements causing acid drainage into streams which kills fish and wildlife. By 1964, more than 800,000 acres of land had been disturbed by strip mining in Appalachia. Spoil banks cut off road access and isolated vast areas from use by people and wildlife. Even more than in the case of timbering, the mining companies find it cheaper to acquire mineral rights to these non-renewable resources than to purchase the land, thus avoiding taxes and escaping the necessity for restoring the land after stripping it of coal.

1. For an excellent appraisal of these problems, see Caudill, 1963.

The tragedy of permanent destruction of the environment is only one aspect of the exploitation of Appalachia by outsiders. The people as well as the physical resources have been exploited by the failure to use adequate shares of the profits from coal and timber exploitation to plow back into the region in the form of investment in human capital.[2] The wealth and power of the coal companies have made it possible for them to dominate local politics, avoid taxation, and escape from restrictive legislation. As a result local schools and other public services have been neglected in Appalachia, depriving the people of education and health services, and leading to cumulative decline in their ability to improve their own lot.

Agriculture in Appalachia, always marginal,has been further damaged by spoil banks, acid mine drainage, soil erosion, and silting of streams. Employment in mining has been cut sharply by mechanization in both underground and surface mining. Consequently, income is low, unemployment high, and the standards of education, health, and housing in Appalachia have been among the lowest in the nation. Nor are the effects confined to Appalachia. Millions of people from Appalachia have migrated, many into the nation's urban areas with very little preparation for urban life, aggravating the other problems of urban centers.

In the short run the national economy benefitted from the apparent low cost of the timber and coal from Appalachia, and while the people of Appalachia have been the primary victims of exploitation of their region, the entire nation will pay a heavy cost in the future for the damage to the natural and human resources of Appalachia. The external diseconomies from mismanagement of regional development, as practiced in Appalachia, are appearing now as real costs in the form of migration of the poor into central cities, and in the form of damage to the land, the scenery, and the water of a vast region. The major objective of the Appalachian program is to correct some of the damage done to the natural and human resources of this region.

Issues

An issue which has never been in serious doubt in Appalachia has been that of aid to a geographic region versus aid to individuals. Here is a region which to an unusual extent illustrates the dynamically interrelated factors of public sector decline and emigration of productive workers in a cumulative process. Failure to reinvest enough of the returns from resource exploitation in local government services had generated cultural

2. In 1962, per pupil expenditure for education was $337 as compared with the national average of $518. The average teacher's salary in Appalachia was $4,200 as compared with the national average of $6,200. See ARC, 1968, p. 48.

entropy and chronic loss of population, so that correction of the process and reestablishment of equilibrium at acceptable levels of activity was impossible without massive outside assistance. In Appalachia there was little debate about the necessity to attack broad regional problems of public services and environmental deterioration as a necessary, if not sufficient, condition to helping the people of the region.

An important issue in the design of the program for Appalachia has been with respect to the role of investment in physical facilties and infrastructure versus investment in human capital programs. There has been widespread recognition of the need for both kinds of programs, but from the beginning heavy emphasis has been placed upon construction of physical facilities, especially roads. The major argument for road building in Appalachia has been that the isolation and lack of transportation and communication make road construction a prerequisite before any other programs can reach the people. There is some merit to this argument, especially for local road systems. However, it is admitted that most of the costly, interstate roads constructed in Appalachia will primarily benefit those areas outside Appalachia, which are provided more efficient and rapid systems for passing through Appalachia without necessarily remaining to spend money in the region. Consequently an additional construction program was added for access roads, though this amounted to only $75 million out of the more than $1 billion authorized for road programs in Appalachia (ARC, 1968, pp. 33-46). There are important contributions that road construction can make in regional development, particularly if the network is carefully designed for development purposes. However, it is questionable whether the major portion of a regional development program should be devoted to roads.

Undoubtedly isolation has been a factor contributing to the overall development problem in Appalachia. However, it is by no means clear that road construction alone will solve the problem. Much of the isolation is a cultural, psychological problem of a people who have sought from the earliest times to escape geographically from Indians, from militiamen, revenue collectors and from the outside world generally. It is much too simplistic an assumption to believe that these problems can be overcome by roads alone for people who may prefer to stay away from roads. Nor is it clear that people who seek isolation should be denied it. The same funds spent on education and cultural programs might do more to break down isolation gradually and voluntarily than could any conceivable road system.

However, the U.S. has traditionally sought to solve difficult social problems by expensive programs of moving earth and pouring concrete. Giving priority to construction and earmarking large sums for this purpose has been the traditional strategy for acquiring the strong support of the construction industry and the political establishments in state and local government for public programs. It is a proven strategy which has worked well in the case of the Appalachian program. Perhaps it has been a necessary price to pay in order to gain acceptance of programs more closely related to the human problems in Appalachia. Unfortunately much of the problem in Appalachia has resulted from abuse of its resources and environment. Road building through mountainous areas, unless carefully planned, can itself cause further environmental damages.

In Appalachia, as in EDA, the issue of concentration versus dispersion of aid has been resolved, in theory at least, in favor of concentration by way of the growth point concept. Under the program, the states are required to identify development districts which are to be 'areas of significant potential for future growth', in the language of the act. These growth centers were to be the primary areas for which public investments would be approved in order to reinforce local capabilities for growth. The administrators of the program have recognized that growth points must have a center or centers as well as hinterlands to which they are connected by economic and physical linkages (M. Newman, 1969). This strategy implies that in allocating aid, as between welfare and efficiency objectives, the welfare, or worst-first priorities would not necessarily be followed if not consistent with growth point strategy. In a sense, the selection of Appalachia for a separate regional program represented a worst-first decision.

Because the Appalachian Region, as defined in the Program, consists of all of West Virginia, and parts of 12 other states, the issue of how much control and planning should occur at each governmental level was a crucial one in designing the program. The final decisions concerning the structure of responsibility represents a new departure in U.S. administration of regional development. The Appalachian program is a joint federal-state program. It is coordinated by the Appalachian Regional Commission, headed by a federal co-chairman, appointed by the president. However, there is also a states' regional representative, appointed by the states. The state governors (or their representatives) serve on the Commission, and elect one of their number as co-chairman. The important operational requirement of the program is that the states propose projects, subject to approval by the Commission. Therefore no action is taken within a state without state approval. However, the Commission is empowered to undertake the planning function and to develop comprehensive, coordinated plans and programs for the entire region.

The Appalachian Regional Commission thus represents another unique stage in the pragmatic U.S. tradition of creating new pluralistic institutions to meet specific regional development needs. In effect, the Appalachian program provides for state autonomy within federal guidelines in planning and administering regional development.

One very important new issue in regional development has been addressed explicitly in the Appalachian program. This issue is the relative importance of environmental factors in regional development. As noted earlier, Appalachia is a region in which short-run exploitation of resources has created external diseconomies and cumulative environmental decline. Resource exploitation based upon leasing of individual resource rights, e.g. to timber or minerals, alienated development from ownership and resulted in failure to treat resources as parts of a total system requiring a systems approach. Purchasers of timber rights stripped the slopes, leaving soil cover to wash onto farms and into streams, in which they had no interest, short run or long run. Purchasers of mineral rights had no long interest in the region, and followed destructive least-cost short-run practices which caused land subsidence, underground fires, spoil banks, scarred surfaces, land slides, acid mine drainage, and water pollution.

Awareness is only beginning to emerge in regional development planning that resource systems are interrelated in complex patterns so that natural resource development requires careful planning in order to avoid irreversible damage to regions and their people. Recognition of this concept can be found in some of the programs provided for in the Appalachian effort. The Appalachian act authorizes the Secretary of the Interior to assist states in filling and sealing abandoned coal mines, reclaiming and rehabilitating areas damaged by surface mining, and extinguishing mine fires. Later amendments to the act provide for study of the economic and social impacts of mine damage pollution. Other programs have been established to assist in preventing land erosion and siltation of water. These are small steps in rehabilitating damaged resources and restoring environmental quality, but they represent an important beginning.

The program

The Appalachian effort goes far beyond earlier regional development programs in the U.S. because it includes the development of comprehensive coordinated plans and programs for the development of the region. ARA and EDA depended primarily upon use of their limited powers to grant or withhold aid to project proposals initiated by public and private groups. The Appalachian Regional Commission has the important power to initiate positive overall plans as a framework within which to allocate its resources and guide other regional development impacts.

Table 2. *Appalachian Regional Development Program: Authorizations and appropriations*

(Thousands of dollars)

Program	Section	Initial authorization fiscal years 65-67	Appropriated fiscal years 65-67	Additional authorization fiscal year 68-69	Cumul. authorization thru 1969[1]	Appropriated fiscal year 1968	Appropriated fiscal year 1969	Total appropriations fiscal years 1965-69
Non-highways:								
Health demonstration	202	69,000	23,500	50,000	73,500	1,400	20,000	44,900
Land stabilization	203	17,000	10,000	19,000	29,000	3,300	2,665	15,965
Timber development	204	5,000	1,000	2,000	3,000	—	—	1,000[2]
Mine area restoration	205	36,500	24,850	30,000	54,850	—	335	25,185[3]
Water resources survey	206	5,000	3,330	2,000	5,330	2,000	—	5,330[4]
Housing fund	207	—	—	5,000	5,000	1,000	1,000	2,000
Vocational education facilities	211	16,000	16,000	26,000	42,000	12,000	14,000	42,000
Sewage treatment	212	6,000	6,000	6,000	12,000	1,400	—	7,400
Supplemental grants	214	90,000	75,000	97,000	172,000	34,000	32,600	141,600
Research and LDD's	302	5,500	5,250	11,000	16,250	1,600	3,000	9,850
Sub-total non-highway		250,000	164,930	248,000	412,930	56,700	73,600	295,230
Less difference in limitations on non-highway appropriations		0	0	—78,000[5]	—78,000	0	0	0
Total non-highway programs		250,000	164,930	170,000	334,930	56,700	73,600	295,230

Program	Section	Initial authorization fiscal years 65-67	Appropriated fiscal years 65-67	Additional authorization fiscal year 68-69	Cumul. authorization thru 1969[1]	Appropriated fiscal year 1968	Appropriated fiscal year 1969	Total appropriations fiscal years 1965-69
Highways	201	840,000	300,000	715,000[6]	1,015,000[1]	70,000	100,000	470,000
Total program cost		1,090,000	464,930	885,000	1,349,930	126,700	173,600	765,230
Administrative expenses	105	2,400	2,390	1,700	4,090	746	850	3,986
Grand total		1,092,400	467,320	886,700	1,354,020	127,446	174,450	769,216

[1] Highway authorization extends through Fiscal Year 1971.
[2] Includes $400 thousand reappropriated to non-Appalachian programs of the Department of Agriculture.
[3] Includes $800 thousand reappropriated to non-Appalachian programs of the Bureau of Mines and Sport Fisheries and Wildlife.
[4] Includes $330 thousand declared as slippage by the Corps of Engineers and thus not available for program.
[5] Total authorizations for non-highway programs were limited to $170 million without specifying where the $78 million difference from program amounts would be taken.
[6] Authorization included $450 million previously authorized but not appropriated and $175 million new authorization.
Source: ARC, 1968, pp. 30-31.

The Appalachian Regional Development Act and its amendments provide for numerous individual programs. Financially the highway program is the most important single part of the Appalachian effort. In fact, expenditures on highways have been substantially greater than the entire rest of the program. As shown in Table 2, the total appropriations for fiscal years 1965 through 1969 for highways were $470 million as compared with $295.2 million (plus $4 million for administration) for all other programs, out of a total of $679 million.[3] However, the act plus amendments authorizes more than $1 billion for eventual highway construction including $75 million for access roads. Construction of 2,700 miles of highway is contemplated. Federal participation of up to 70 percent of the total cost is allowed.

As a supplemental transportation program another $93.4 million was authorized for airport construction. It is difficult to visualize extensive direct benefits from an aviation program to the unemployed and underemployed of Appalachia. The authorization of this amount of money for airports in a regional poverty program clearly indicates the tendency to expand programs which would be difficult to justify on their own merits by rationalizing them as aspects of programs developed for other high priority national objectives.

But to a greater extent than any previous U.S. program for regional development, the program for Appalachia recognizes the need to deal with the fundamental human problems which depress the quality of life in a region. The Commission demonstrated an early understanding of the significance not only of the traditional economic indicators dealing with income and unemployment, but also of the new concern with more general social indicators (see, for example, Olsen, 1969). For example, in assessing the needs for the region, it has been noted that as compared with the national average, Appalachian residents receive lower expenditures per pupil for education, have lower teachers' salaries, lower mental test scores, higher disease rates, and higher infant mortality (ARC, 1968, p. 48).

In its program for improving the conditions of life in Appalachia, the Commission appropriately gives education a high priority. For the years 1965 through 1969, $42 million was appropriated for this purpose, mostly for vocational education. Unfortunately, it is difficult to add on a successful vocational education program to an educational system which does not provide a strong primary and secondary school background upon which to build. Recent findings about importance of nutrition and education in the very early years suggest that successful improvement of the quality

3. This comparison is complicated by the fact that the highway authorization runs through 1971.

of education in Appalachia and other regions of deprivation will require drastic revision of education programs at all levels, beginning at preschool levels. Recent Appalachian programs in childhood development are based upon an awareness of these problems.

Health programs have also been an important part of the federal efforts to aid Appalachian development. A total of $44.9 million was appropriated from 1965 through 1969 for health demonstration projects. These funds are used for planning, constructing, equipping, and operating health facilities. Matching funds from other federal and local sources are required in these projects. In order to staff the facilities, other programs have been designed to train health personnel and upgrade their skills. These are programs which directly address the personal problems which prevent persons from becoming productive members of society. Creation of jobs alone cannot benefit those who are too ill or too poorly educated to seek and hold jobs.

Additional programs to improve the quality of life in Appalachia have included efforts to provide better housing. Appropriations of $2 million have been used primarily to provide technical assistance and cover some of the local costs of participating in existing national housing programs.

Among the most important and most innovative of the Appalachian programs have been those to improve natural resource use and to improve environmental quality. The cost to future generations of destructive resource exploitation is very high. In making only a modest initial effort at correcting some of the past damage created by short-run exploitation of mineral resources, the Appalachian program has appropriated more than $25 million to extinguish underground coal fires which have damaged large areas, seal off abandoned mines, correct land subsidence, and rehabilitate land damaged by surface mining. The appropriations are minute in relationship to the total amount of damaged areas to be rehabilitated, and to date have been limited in use only to areas where future economic development prospects are favorable. Additional programs are underway to study the effects and possible remedies for drainage of acids and other pollutants from mining areas into waterways.

Water pollution in Appalachia originates not only from mine drainage but from sewage. Appropriations to deal with this problem have amounted to $7.4 million, mostly from supplemental assistance under existing federal water pollution control programs. The problem of land stabilization and soil erosion has been approached by providing almost $16 million for cost sharing with farmers under the existing U.S. Department of Agriculture conservation program.

One of the most important of the Appalachian natural resource programs is the allocation of $5.3 million for a water resources survey. This is a regional study of the effects that water management can have on economic development, and is intended to result in a water development plan for the entire region. However, potential problems which may be circumvented are inherent in the fact that the study was originally intended to emphasize the maximum contribution the water resources of the region can make to development rather than to emphasize water as a basic resource within a larger system of natural resources and environmental quality.

Aside from highways, which have absorbed more than half of the total funds available for Appalachian regional development, the largest single budget category has been for supplemental grants, which accounted for $141.6 million from 1965 through 1969. These are funds which have been provided to help make up the local government share of funds normally required for local participation in federal sharing programs. In recognition of the cumulative decline in the capacity of local governments in the region, funds are provided under this program to help Appalachian communities overcome their severe competitive disavantage with other more rigorous local governments in competing for participation in these programs. The largest programs involved have been for higher education ($26.6. million), Hill-Burton Act for assistance to hospitals ($25.3 million), vocational education ($23 million), and water pollution control ($13.2 million). These funds have also been used for libraries, airports, scholarships, water supply, educational television, and other programs discussed above. The size of this program demonstrates the tendency in U.S. regional development programs to work where possible with existing programs and to use facilities of other agencies to administer elements of the program.

Local planning functions are performed under the Appalachian program by local development districts, which are multi-county regions designed to pool local resources of several counties in order to achieve higher levels of specialization and skill than would be available to smaller units in depressed areas. The local development districts are intended to provide a bridge between local and state governments as the Appalachian Commission does between the federal and state governments. Staffing was originally provided by the Commission but will eventually be state financed. Funds totalling $9.8 million were appropriated for this purpose and for the research function.

The programs of the Appalachian Regional Commission have been strengthened by a highly effective research program. The research efforts have been focused sharply upon providing a common set of regional data and upon assisting states to develop concrete investment programs within each development district. The program has emphasized applied rather than basic research, and is intended to be relevant to specific planning needs in the development districts. Individual research studies under the program have included industry location factors, opportunities for employment in service activities, relationships of local governments to development, availability of private and public capital, and development potentials of specific regions.

Evaluation

The accomplishments of the Appalachian program within its short period of existence have been impressive. In terms of economic conditions there is partial and inconclusive evidence that the large gap between Appalachia and the rest of the nation is narrowing slightly. Employment rates are increasing in the region somewhat faster than in the nation, and rates of unemployment and out-migration appear to be falling (Widner, 1969, II, pp. 1-6). Personal per capita incomes appear to be rising slightly faster than those for the nation (ARC, 1968, p. 6). Of course, it is impossible to estimate how much of this regional economic improvement is directly attributable to the Appalachian program, and how much improvement would have occurred in its absence.

In addition to the economic improvement, the Commission staff is convinced that coordination between federal, state, and local governments has improved with the adoption of local planning districts and the use of state plans to coordinate a broad range of assistance programs. Plans and research have been completed for transport networks, water resource programs, land reclamation, recreation programs, education programs, and health programs. More than 1,000 public facilities proposals have been approved (Jones and Widner, 1969). A beginning has been made, but there is general agreement that much more remains to be done if Appalachia is to be given the opportunity to participate fully in the main stream of U.S. economic development. The Appalachian regional development program, as an evolutionary step in the U.S. experience with regional development, has been hampered by the limitations of traditional thinking about these problems, but has also demonstrated some promising innovations which are suggestive of the wave of the future in regional development.

The aspect of the program which has attracted most criticism has been the very heavy priority given to road construction. Although valid arguments have been advanced to support the highway program, the allocation of more than 60 percent of total appropriations for this purpose suggests that the critics have a point. The large airport program raises even more questions about priorities. Very carefully designed benefit-cost studies to compare highway programs with the alternative human development programs are needed to cast more light on this problem. this

Major problems of the Appalachian program are finding more effective methods for coordinating its efforts with local governments and with other federal agencies. For example, the strong insistence by the Appalachian Commission on limiting its assistance to areas with growth potential in order to emphasize productivity is in conflict with the EDA worst first strategy of emphasizing welfare. Both of these objectives, productivity and welfare, are important, and more explicit coordination between the two is needed. Coordination with some state governments has been more successful than with others and continuing efforts are needed in this direction. Some states have been slow to develop planning and research capabilities. The requirement that proposals must originate with states is both an advantage and a disadvantage, depending upon the capabilities of the individual states involved.

Administration of the program might be improved if fragmentation of states could be avoided. Where only parts of states are included, planning for Appalachian areas of the state could be improved if coordinated with planning for the rest of the state, even though not all of the state would be eligible for aid under Appalachian program requirements.

Excessive family size is an additional and fundamental problem in parts of Appalachia. This is a sensitive issue which it may be effective to treat at low levels of publicity and discussion. But as a human problem it deserves very high priority, and much effort should be devoted to finding culturally and politically acceptable programs for family planning for those who want them. The potential payoff in both human and economic values from family planning programs is great enough to merit much more effort.

Among the greatest achievements of the Appalachia program are the innovations in cooperative federal-state-local planning for regional development. This planning effort has departed significantly from earlier U.S. program which have been primarily passive, permissive programs of reacting to proposals. The Appalachian effort breaks new ground in developing specific physical designs for regional development which provide concrete guidelines for coordinating development facilities. Important innovations have been made in tailoring plans to the specific needs of individual areas.

Other major achievements of the Appalachian program have been to break away from the traditional dependence upon attempting to aid individuals through the market processes and to substitute specific programs to invest in human capabilities and to improve the quality of life and environment in the region. An implicit assumption of the program is that in aiding chronically ill, unemployed, untrained persons to become productive, it is more cost-effective to upgrade their capabilities than to create new jobs which they are unlikely to be able to fill without prior assistance.

Appalachian efforts to correct the extensive physical damage to the environment of the region from destructive methods of natural resource exploitation deserve careful study. They underline the importance of improved resource management and environmental planning in order to prevent costly future programs of correction, and to prevent irreversible environmental damage. The Appalachian experience emphasizes systems relationships between economic, social, and environmental factors that are becoming crucial with rising levels of population and economic development.

CHAPTER X

Other multi-state regional commissions

Introduction

As in the case of many U.S. regional development programs, the establishment of the Appalachian Regional Commission quickly led to the organization of similar projects to serve other multi-state regions. The Public Works and Economic Development Act of 1965 (Title V, Public Law 89-136), in addition to establishing the Economic Development Administration, had also provided for the establishment of regional commissions to aid those multi-state regions in which economic development lagged behind that of the national average. Thus far, five of these additional regional commissions have been established. They are:

- The Ozarks Regional Commission (parts of Arkansas, Oklahoma, Kansas, and Missouri)
- The Four Corners Regional Commission (parts of Arizona, Colorado, New Mexico, and Utah)
- The Coastal Plains Regional Commission (parts of Georgia, North Carolina, and South Carolina)
- The Upper Great Lakes Regional Commission (parts of Michigan, Minnesota, and Wisconsin)
- The New England Regional Commission (all of Connecticut, Maine, Massachusetts, New Hampshire, Rhode Island, and Vermont)

In concept, the regional commissions are closest in U.S. regional development experience to the Appalachian Regional Commission. The latter, however, was established under a separate and independent administration, while the regional commissions are all administered under the Office of Regional Development Planning (ORDP) within EDA. The important feature of these regional commissions is that, like the Appalachian effort, they represent a new federal-state approach to the solution of uniquely regional problems. The specific regional focus of these five commissions has revealed both a core of traditional problems common to all lagging areas of the nation, as well as some uniquely new local approaches to values, objectives, issues, and programs in regional economic development.

Values

While the operations of the five regional commissions do reveal local variations in values, priorities, and style, their establishment reflects the traditional U.S. beliefs that have had continuity in the national approach to this problem. They reflect the belief in the right of all individuals, and hence of all regions, to pursue their objectives, particularly pursuit of affluence and development. Establishment of the five commissions also reflects the national confidence in the ability to innovate new institutions for particular purposes, and if they prove successful, or even promising, to proliferate these institutions and programs in other areas. The regional commissions further underline the pragmatic, pluralistic, federal approach to cooperation between various levels of government with private sector participation. However, the regional implementation of these shared values has generated a wide degree of local variation and emphasis.

Objectives

The major objectives of the regional commissions have been to reduce local economic distress and to reduce the lag between local and national levels of economic achievement. The regional commissions have been highly specific in identifying and measuring the differences between per capita income within their regions as compared with the national average, and in quantifying the size of this divergence as a total income gap to be eliminated.

As shown in Table 3, the estimated annual income gaps per capita, for the three regions which have published these figures, range from $700 in the Four Corners to $1,000 in the Ozarks. The estimated annual totals of income gaps for the regions run as high as $5.3 billion for the Coastal Plains. Reducing the magnitude of these income gaps and the job gaps which are associated with them constitutes a highly specific and quantifiable set of objectives for these regions. It is of interest to note that in New England, where per capita incomes are higher than the national average (and thus the income gap is negative), objectives are stated in terms of raising incomes in the lower income areas of the region towards the regional average.

The pursuit of these development objectives by the regional commissions has indicated an emerging consensus on some of the traditional issues in the U.S. approach to regional development, and has advanced the recognition of new issues yet to be resolved. Some of these issues and their shifting priorities are examined in following sections.

Table 3. *Regional income gaps*

Region	Year	Per capita gap	Total gap
Ozarks	1967	$1,000	$2.7 billion
Four Corners	1967	$ 700	$1.5
Coastal Plains	1965	$ 977	$5.3

Sources: ORC, 1969, p. 8; FCRC, 1969, pp. 4-5; CPRC, 1968, pp. 21-24.

Issues

Establishment of the regional commissions further confirms the acceptance in the U.S. of the concept of attempting to aid people through the device of providing aid to a region and assuming that needy persons will eventually benefit from those programs. The validity of this concept is challenged by the growing concern that traditional U.S. regional development programs by their very nature provide benefits primarily to less needy and more affluent, by channelling funds into construction companies for public sector facilities and into business firms for aid to the private sector.

However, some of the inconsistency of this approach may be reduced by the growing recognition and admission of the fact that regional economic development does not necessarily alleviate poverty, nor do anti-poverty programs necessarily lead to long-run self-sustaining regional economic development. Recognition of the need for two separate types of programs each finely tuned to achieve its separate (though admittedly related) set of objectives may lead to improved allocation of funds between these two kinds of programs. This kind of recognition appears to be emerging in budget requests of the regional commissions with their separate proposals for funds for investment in human capital as well as for the traditional public works and aid to private business.

A related issue is that of regional economic development versus general regional development. Evaluation of some of the annual reports of the regional commissions indicates an awareness of the fact that regional economic development cannot be achieved in isolation, but that it is one aspect of general regional development which requires more than simple investment in the public and private sectors of the regional economy.

Emphasis must also be given to regional entrepreneurial capabilities, environmental quality, cultural values, quality of local government, social justice, and related phenomena, if satisfactory levels of economic development are to be achieved.

The issue of concentration versus dispersion of regional development effort appears to have been resolved at least in principle in favor of concentration with general acceptance of the growth point concept by the regional commissions. The concept of efficiency rather than equity has been adopted with commitment to the principle of obtaining maximum development per dollar of expenditure. Thus, even where expenditures are to be made for investment in human capital, priority is nominally to be given to those areas with greatest growth potential.

An improved basis for the application of the growth point principle has been provided by research sponsored by the Upper Great Lakes Commission in a comprehensive report prepared by Brian L. J. Berry (1969). In his proposal for the Upper Great Lakes Regions, Berry emphasizes the importance of selecting centers which have potential for growth because of their linkages with a productive hinterland. Berry points out that the existence of a growth center is of major importance to its hinterland and to broader regions because development and innovation usually begin in urban centers and spread throughout the region. He bases his analysis on the concept of hierarchies of city size and function, in which the largest centers provide not only economic services but cultural and intellectual stimuli which diffuse down through networks of smaller satellite centers and throughout the region. Berry's work is based upon explicit analysis of spatial relationships and functional linkages between distances and sizes of centers in the regional economic network. His functional analysis of economic space in the Upper Great Lakes permits him to identify growth areas, peripheral zones, slow growth areas, and lagging regions. On the basis of the linkages and spread effects between these regions, he has been able to design a detailed spatial development plan for the region which identifies specific primary growth centers, secondary growth centers, service centers, and zones of influence of these centers as well as areas having significant tourist-recreation growth potentials. Given necessary limitations upon the total funds available for aiding regional development, allocating these funds into areas having realistic growth potential is much more likely to yield lasting developmental benefits than unselective dispersion of the funds into areas with weaker economic linkages.

Among the new regional development issues being given greater emphasis in the deliberations of the regional commissions is that of economic growth versus environmental quality. Despite the general reluctance to accept the basic fact that economic development necessarily creates environmental modification and usually creates environmental degradation, recognition is growing that environmental protection measures should be written into economic development plans before costly, irreversible environmental damage occurs.

One of the most forthright confrontations of the conflict between growth and environmental quality can be found in the deliberations of the New England Regional Commission. The Commission's draft report (1969) goes farther than most public documents in recognizing candidly that dense urban population growth has caused external costs in terms of contaminated air and water, traffic congestion, inadequate open and recreation space, and other problems. Facing the implications of its analysis, in a reversal of the usual configuration of the north-south problem, the Commission recommends a strategy of controlling growth in the congested southern New England states and encouraging growth in the less developed northern states in order to promote an open and clean environment. It is unusual to find recognition in print of the need to control growth even as between areas within political subdivisions, and of the need to reallocate growth between political subdivisions.

One of the newest issues in regional development to emerge in the debates associated with the regional commissions is that over the desirability of exempting distressed regions from certain national regulations, and giving special treatment to these regions. Historically, the nation has set up programs of special aid to lagging regions above and beyond aid available to the rest of the nation, but there has been little precedent for relaxing national standards or reducing statutory requirements on the basis of regional development. Under certain circumstances the Department of Defense is permitted to set aside some procurement contracts for areas of economic distress, but the actual effects of these regulations have been negligible (U.S. 1967).

A break with this tradition is found in the proposals of some of the regional commissions for granting the lagging regions relaxation of federal tax regulations, increasing tax concessions, reducing national interest rate regulations, and relaxing federal regulatory requirements. For example, the Coastal Plains Regional Commission (1968, pp. 44-53) points out that national policies for price stability and inflation control may adversely affect lagging regions where employment of underemployed resources would not necessarily add to inflationary pressures. It therefore recommends consideration of special treatment for lagging regions in the form of selective exemption from the personal surtax, interest rate increases, corporate income tax, depreciation allowances, tax write-offs, and in establishing preferential interest rates, interest subsidies, loan and reserve requirements, regulatory devices, transport rates licensing and inspection procedures, labor policies, production controls, port regulations, and planning and zoning regulations.

These proposals raise the additional issue of the relationship between possible conflicts between regional and national objectives. Proposals of the regional commission envisage elimination of special treatment if and when regional parity is attained, and recommend a national study of the proposals. Implicit in the arguments of the regional commissions is the assumption that regional development, especially if it increases the use of otherwise underemployed regional resources does not necessarily come at the expense of other regions or reduce national growth. That is, it assumes that regional development is not a zero-sum game.

This new issue is clearly an important one. The fact that it has also been discussed by the Upper Great Lakes Regional Commission (1969, p. 8) indicates that it will probably receive increasing attention. Proposals to make an independent national study of this approach to regional assistance are well worth adopting. It would be valuable to determine under what circumstances, if any, relaxation of national legislation and regulations could advance regional objectives without injuring other regions or the nation.

The assertion that these special concessions to lagging regions need not impair national objectives neglects the fact of interregional linkages. For example, in times of inflationary pressure, increased investment in lagging regions could occur without adding to inflationary pressures only if it resulted in employing regional resources for which there was no competing demand in the region or outside it, and if resulting indirect and secondary demands for inputs could be supplied by previously unemployed or underemployed resources from within the region or from other regions.

Proposals to reduce national regulatory standards on environmental quality regulations in distressed regions raise the problem of regional externalities. Lagging regions are under competitive pressure to relax air and water quality standards, but air and water pollution do not stop at political boundaries. The fact that regional competition in resource mismanagement is not in the national or regional interest was a prime reason for establishing federal regulation in these fields, after a difficult struggle, originally. To relax them would be a serious blow to the public interest.

In a dynamic context, it is difficult to see how any initial concessions to regional economies could ever be eliminated. Despite agreements to stop special concessions once parity had been attained, there is the problem that if special concessions were required to begin with to make a project viable in an otherwise unfavorable environment, it would be unlikely ever to achieve competitive status. Special subsidies should probably not be granted if they would be required permanently, and if they were not guaranteed on a permanent basis, they might not be effective at all. In this respect they are similar to infant industry arguments for tariff concessions.

Persistent historical trends in U.S. regional development suggest that any relaxation of national standards in one region tends to result in pressures for unselective proliferation of programs into all regions. Indeed, constitutional and legal provisions sanction proliferation, or equal treatment. Introduction of regional concessions in tax and other national regulations might thus lead to competitive pressures for proliferation. Potential administrative problems and questions of constitutionality are also involved. In this respect, current U.S. policy of adding new programs and specific assistance to lagging regions has much to commend it over programs for selective relaxation of federal regulations. The incremental addition of new programs for regional development based upon added expenditures in these regions also has the advantage that the size and distribution of the subsidies involved is easily visible and measurable. However, by contrast, selective relaxation of tax or other regulations involves subsidies whose magnitude and distribution are less visible and quantifiable, and whose direct and indirect effects are much less predictable.

The important question to arise from this issue is what kinds of interregional competition are likely to result in constructive outcomes for both regions and the nation. Competition in reducing regional environmental standards, in increasing subsidies to encourage industrial relocation and competition in maximizing regional relaxation of national standards would be difficult to justify from the viewpoint of overall growth and national allocation of scarce resources. Conversely, interregional competition in improving environmental quality, in improving human skills, in raising productivity, and in improving the quality of regional development would benefit both the region and the nation. Setting the rules of the game to encourage interregional competition to maximize external economies and to minimize external diseconomies where possible would be in the interest of the nation and of the region. There are important opportunities and challenges for increased research in the search for non-zero sum games in interregional economic competition. From both the national and regional points of view, the objective should be to improve the quality of economic development as it affects the lives of people in the regions, rather than to aim merely at maximizing growth rates, which may deteriorate the quality of environment and life (Mishan, 1967).

The issue of how to define an appropriate region is yet to be resolved in the establishment of the regional commissions. All except New England involve parts of states in multi-state regions. Most regional commissions are based upon complete counties as building blocks, but one (Four Corners) even includes part of a county as well as 91 full counties. The problem of defining development regions, especially for multi-state regions, will be a pressing one, since the probabilities are high that pressures for participation in these programs will spread to other states. This outcome is suggested both by the history of economic development programs in the U.S. and by the fact that a regional commission has been established for New England, which, though hardly one of the nation's lower income areas, does have pockets of economic distress and other problems, along with its traditionally innovative, adaptable growth centers. The concept of establishing special development regions to meet uniquely regional problems, circumstances, objectives, and approaches is a reasonable one. It is also clear that problems of resource management, transport nets and environmental design do not stop at the boundaries of states, which are suboptimal in size for dealing with many aspects of regional development in a technological society.

If, as appears likely, regional development commissions are set up for other groups of states, eventually including all states, they could provide one basis for design of a national plan for regional development. One of the many implications of such a possibility is a strengthening of the argument for including all of the counties of a state within the definition of the multi-state region. Another implication is that between such sets of multi-state regions, there are interrelationships such as competition and economic flows which will become more important and more in need of explicit analysis. For example, the question may well arise whether a state should be permitted to be a part of more than one regional commission, whether regional commissions might overlap, or whether parts of states might be divided between more than one regional commission.

Programs

The programs of the regional commissions to date have varied widely in the quality of research and planning. It is possible here to list only a few highlights of each.

The Ozarks Regional Commission. The Ozarks Commission has thus far under a limited program given top priority to overcoming deficiencies in educational structure, and it has chosen to begin by building and equipping technical education centers in Missouri and Oklahoma, and by designing an education information system in Arkansas. The individual states have prepared investment programs for economic development to be used by the Commission in designing a regional development plan. The Ozarks Regional Commission (1968, p. 33) recognizes that the emerging scarcity value of open space may provide this region with its greatest opportunities for the future, but significant improvements in infrastructure and the quality of local government services will be essential if immigrants are to be attracted to the unspoiled areas of this region in the future.

The Four Corners Regional Commission. This huge region comprises 8 percent of the total U.S. land mass. It contains large Indian reservations and much of the land is federally owned. Perhaps its greatest challenges and opportunities exist in efforts to undertake constructive programs to meet the needs of the Indians in the region. An important issue emerges here from the fact that it is difficult to encourage economic development without appearing to impose the white man's values upon Indian cultural values and heritage. Much sensitivity and wisdom are necessary in designing plans which can increase the number of options open to Indians without alienating them from their culture and destroying their society. In this kind of problem, the participation of anthropologists, historians, psychologists, and sociologists is at least as important as the insight of economists. For example, recent proposals have been made by the Westinghouse Corporation to construct a $1 billion new town in this region where the reservations of the Navaho and Ute Indians join (*U.S.* 1969). If assistance to the Indians is a major objective of this project, it would be useful to examine benefit-cost ratios of alternative projects which would be more consistent with the cultural values and environmental resources of the region.

The Commission has identified its priorities as improvement of transportation, education and health, agriculture, mineral production, and industry (FCRC, 1969). It has accepted the principle of concentrating its efforts at potential growth centers, in addressing its major objectives of closing its income gap by creating 30,000 new jobs per year (Brewer, 1969).

The Coastal Plains Regional Commission. The Coastal Plains Commission has adopted a comprehensive approach to regional planning, which explicitly provides for recognition of national goals, regional goals, progress indicators (the increasingly popular concept of the income gap), dependent variable (private investment), target variable, policy variables, policy decisions and policy administration. A chart of the relationships between these concepts is shown in Figure 1 which is structured in terms of the development strategy of the Commission. The Coastal Plains Commission has recognized its major needs in the area of human capital

Figure 1. Strategy for development of the Coastal Plains Region

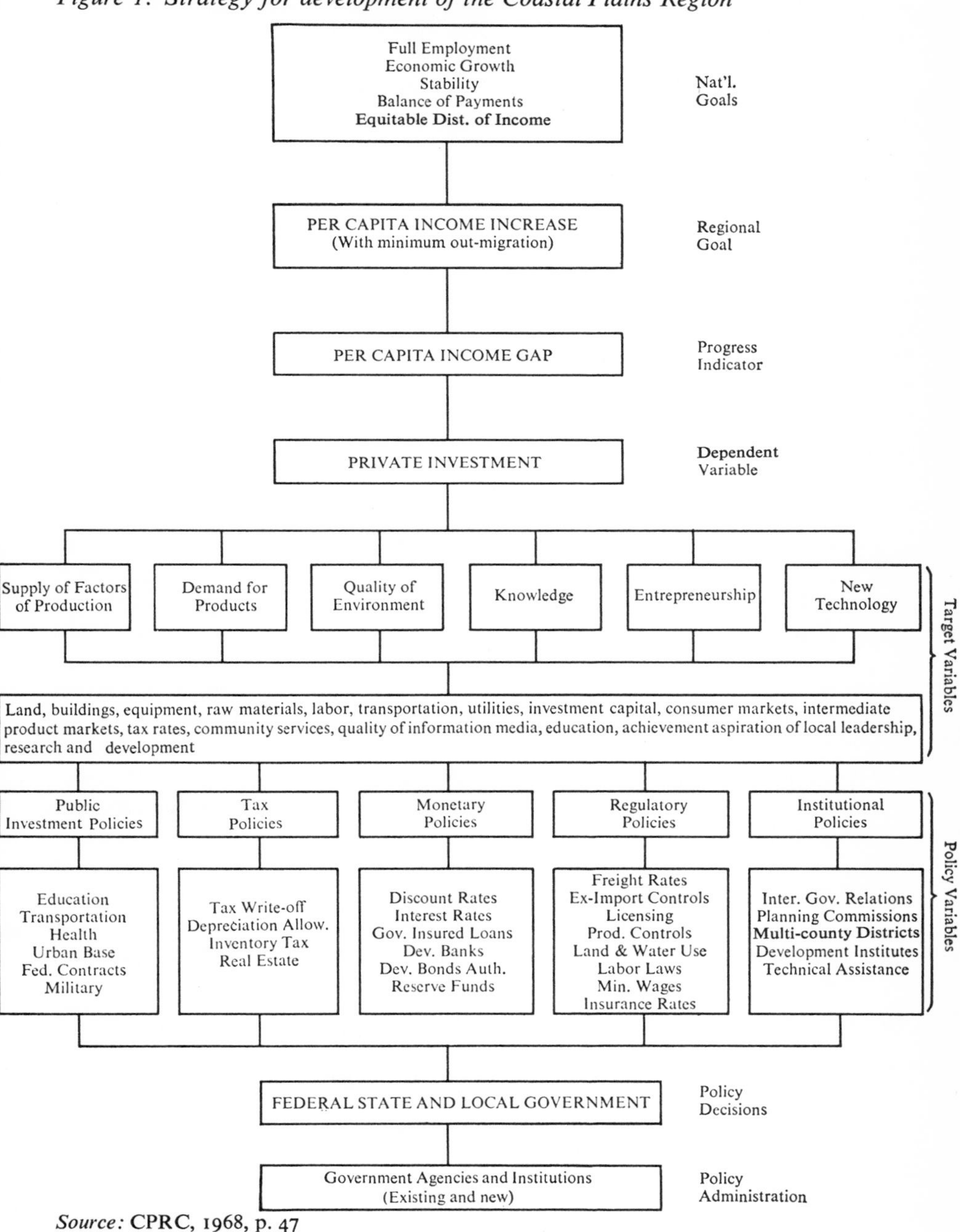

Source: CPRC, 1968, p. 47

investment (Flora, 1968). Its budget proposals emphasize investment in vocational education, manpower training, as well as development of marine resources, agriculture, forestry, tourism and recreation, and industrial development. However, out of a proposed budget of approximately $167 million, including federal and state contributions, by far the largest portion, $115, almost 70 percent is proposed for highway construction (CPRC, 1968, p. 89). Despite recognition of the human capital problem, the spending proposals of the Commission put overwhelming emphasis upon creation of physical capital, concentrated in a single sector, highway construction.

The Coastal Plains Regional Commission has been a leader in advocating relaxation of federal regulations and standards as assistance measures to lagging regions, as discussed above. The existence of a regional income gap estimated at more than $5 billion annually goes far in explaining the concern about federal fiscal, monetary and other policies which impinge heavily upon this region. However, pursuit of the policies proposed would raise severe problems of conflict between regional and national objectives for which no remedies have been proposed but which might be avoided by alternative programs aimed at raising the quality of development in lagging regions, rather than by attempting to modify the impact of federal standards by regions.

The Coastal Plains Regional Commission (1968, p. 247) recognizes that failure to achieve intensive early industrial development has some advantages, in leaving options open for the future, and in giving the region the opportunity to adopt air and water quality standards before pollution has reached irreversible proportions.

The Upper Great Lakes Regional Commission. The Upper Great Lakes Commission has taken the important early step of providing a comprehensive research basis for designing its development plan. The study by Berry (1969) has provided an analysis of the entire economic space of the region with its hierarchies of different city size, measurement of linkages and delineation of hinterlands. This analysis has provided the basis for concentrating public investment and planning efforts into these areas which have maximum potential as primary growth centers, secondary growth centers, service centers, and tourist-recreation growth areas. This research effort, closely attuned to the policy decision problems and operating needs of the program, has provided the Upper Great Lakes Regional Commission with a sophisticated extension of the growth center concept and with an authoritative basis for long-range regional economic development planning.

In addition to its efforts to provide for physical-economic planning, the

Upper Great Lakes Commission has indicated an awareness of the critical role that natural resource management and environmental relationships will play in this region. The lakes of the region are being treated as a system of waterways within larger systems of resources, and emphasis has been given to reducing pollution in the lakes, restoring the health of fish populations, protection of amenities, expanding the park system, and encouraging year-round tourism and recreation. However, conflicts with these environmental objectives may emerge from other proposals in the region to encourage the growth of pulp and paper operations and production of pelletized iron ore. These operations entail large-scale materials processing and are highly pollution intensive. Unless new technologies can be designed which approach environmental neutrality in their operating characteristics, heavy materials processing is hardly consistent with achievement of environmental quality and protection of amenities.

However, the releases of the Commission do indicate an awareness of the dangers of environmental damage. The Commission also indicated its concern for relating its programs to national growth and welfare, even to the extent of accepting migration out of the region.[1] Reconciliation of the Commission's concern for environmental quality with its interest in pulp and iron pellet production, and reconciling its concern for the national interest with its interest in selective regional relaxation of federal fiscal and other regulations will present definite challenges in the design of regional development plans.

The New England Regional Commission. The program of the New England Commission is of particular interest because it is being designed not for an underdeveloped, lagging region, but for an advanced, industrialized region with its own set of problems. The statements of the Commission suggest an awareness that some of its areas actually suffer from overdevelopment, especially in the congested industrial cities of southern, New England. An explicit objective of the Commission, reflecting a rare political courage, is to channel more development opportunities into the sparsely developed northern part of New England.

In addressing the problems unique to the region, the Commission has expressed concern over high energy costs as a barrier to development. In this connection, the proposal to construct a petroleum refinery and free port at Machiasport in Maine raises the issue that is increasingly faced by all industrial regions of balancing economic development with probable environmental deterioration. Proposals to construct a similar free port

1. Upper Great Lakes Regional Commission, Statement of Harold C. Jordahl, Jr., March 6, 1969.

and refinery in tidewater Southern Mayland have been opposed because of local preference for foregoing the possible short-run economic advantages in favor of maintaining high environmental quality in the long run. A benefit-cost study of the refinery proposal indicated that if the refinery were built, the limited tax and income advantages would be far exceeded by long-run damage from possible oil spills and other environmental effects if these problems reduced the growth rates of existing seafood, recreation, and tourist activities by only a small percentage of their expected growth rates (see Dodge and Cumberland, 1970).

High energy costs and growing energy requirements have also confronted New England with the problems associated with nuclear energy. Increasing evidence suggests that the rush into nuclear energy is occurring before some of the critical problems of nuclear contamination and thermal waste have been adequately understood and solved. Debate over this issue has been extensive in the New England region and in the nation.[2] Earlier limited concern about the direct nuclear and thermal effects of nuclear power stations is yielding to broader questioning about the total systems effect of the nuclear power industry, including the effects upon uranium miners, effects of radioactive sedimentation from mine spoil runoff into waterways, flow of radioactive pollution waste products from nuclear fuel manufacturing, accident hazards in transportation of nuclear fuel, and the long term hazards to the earth's environment from long-lasting nuclear wastes and their leakage into the atmosphere, water supplies, underground aquifers, waterways, and oceans. Failure to examine the total benefits and costs of nuclear technology as a complete system has led to an excessively rapid and heavily subsidized rush into the widespread application of nuclear energy before adequate measures have been designed for environmental protection against nuclear and thermal damage from atomic plants. This competitive drive for nuclear energy poses a particularly difficult dilemma for a region like New England, which suffers from high energy costs. A comprehensive national policy for regional development would include specific plans for design and development of a national power grid and analysis of full social and economic benefits and costs of alternative plant sites and technologies to meet future energy requirements.

2. Harry Foreman (ed.), *Nuclear Power and the Public*, Minneapolis, University of Minnesota Press, 1971; *Man's Impact on the Global Environment*, Report of the Study of Critical Environmental Problems (SCEP), Cambridge, Mass., The MIT press, 1970; Office of Science and Technology, *Electric Power and Environment*, Washington, D. C., Energy Policy Staff, U.S. Government Printing Office, August 1970; Library of Congress, *The Economy, Energy and the Environment*, Policy Division of the Legislative Service, Washington, D. C., September 1970; Bernard Udis (ed.), *Adjustments of the U.S. Economy to Reductions in Military Spending*, United States Arms Control and Disarmament Agency, ACDA/E156, Washington, D. C., December 1970.

The environmental problems faced by an advanced industrial region are also illustrated by the attempts of the New England region to dispose of its expanding waste load by means of waste disposal in the ocean. A five year study by Harvard and the University of Rhode Island proposed waste incineration and dumping in 100 to 200 foot depths of the ocean. However, reports of preliminary results of another study by the U.S. Bureau of Sports Fisheries and Wildlife are not nearly as favorable and suggest that even deep sea deposits of sludge from waste disposal may be detrimental to marine environment and to beach ecology and use (SFI, 1969). Early warnings that even the oceans, long regarded as an ultimate and inexhaustible sink for human waste, are becoming polluted emphasize the conflict between economic development and environmental preservation, and underline the urgency of developing technologies which are more environmentally neutral.

Evaluation

As the most recent set of programs in the evaluation of U.S. experience in regional development, the regional commissions illustrate both the emergence of new issues and priorities as well as the weight of historical experience and tradition. The commissions have broken new ground in the pragmatic design of flexible institutions for addressing current issues. They offer new opportunities for groups of states to coordinate their plans and to confront federal agencies. Their objective of obtaining maximum development per dollar of expenditure is resulting in innovative research on the nature of growth centers and hinterlands. The focus upon regional objectives has led to increased concern for achieving high levels of environmental quality as a goal of comparable importance with traditional concern for maximizing regional growth. A new awareness is emerging concerning the need for research on technologies and patterns of spatial development which will permit continued economic development with minimum environmental damage. The regional commissions have indicated a new willingness to consider the difficult questions of encouraging interregional migration and of actually slowing down growth rates in 'overdeveloped' areas.

The regional orientation of the commissions has encouraged searching analyses of uniquely local development problems and the evaluation of programs specifically tailored to local variations in problem areas. For example, the New England Commission faces the problems of an advanced high-technology industrialized region. The region historically has innovated in creation of new technologies and new high-skill industries and has lost them to other regions as the industries mature, become routinized and are attracted to low-wage regions. The shoe and textile industries are examples. Other problems faced in New England are the congestion and environmental deterioration of long-industrialized urban concentrations. In facing these problems, the New England Regional Commission has been willing to recognize the needs for reducing growth rates in the urbanized south and channelling more development options and migration to less developed northern states. It has also recognized the urgency of arresting environmental decline and improving the quality of environmental management in the region.

By contrast, the other regional commissions have dealt with more traditional problems of underinvestment in human resources and mismanagement of natural resources. Efforts are being made to assist the Indians in the Upper Great Lakes Region and the Four Corners Region, and to compensate for the damage to blacks resulting from generations of share-cropping practices in the Coastal Plains.

However, despite these advances, the effectiveness of the programs of the regional commissions are jeopardized by the persistence of some of the traditional U.S. approaches to regional development which may not be as appropriate today as they were in earlier periods. The budget proposals of some of the commissions give major emphasis to spending upon construction of highways and physical facilities rather than upon efforts to eliminate more fundamental obstacles to regional development. The emerging demands for selective relaxation of federal regulations for taxes, interest rates, and other national standards to assist lagging regions raise troublesome questions about incentives to encourage inefficiency and the perpetuation of regional lags.

Perhaps the greatest needs of the regional commissions are to provide the research and data base for designing development plans with specific, quantified, time-phased objectives and for making benefit-cost studies of alternative programs for achievement of these objectives. New methods of Program Planning and Budgeting Systems (PPBS) offer promising techniques for moving towards the efficient design and administration of regional development programs. However, their implementation will require, both at the regional and the national levels, more extensive data especially on interregional flows, improved systems of regional social accounts, and greatly expanded research programs and staffs.

CHAPTER XI

The special case of Alaska

The future economic development of Alaska will provide a critical testing ground for U.S. regional development theory and practice. It is here that the demands of the future for fuel and economic expansion will confront all of the traditional issues in regional development. But in addition, more recent conflicts in contemporary U.S. values are emerging in Alaska on a very large scale.

In many ways, Alaska combines all of the important characteristics of the historical frontier in America. Its vast expanses (586,000 square miles) are dominated by a harsh environment with which its native Eskimos and Indians had worked out a viable ecological balance. However, the attraction of the wilderness and of great potential wealth from resource exploitation has attracted a half million white settlers, most of whom are eager to get on with the business of conquering this environment and modifying it in order to exploit its resources. As on earlier frontiers, they view their priorities as utilizing public sector financial support to provide the transportation and other infrastructure systems needed to facilitate private sector development. As in the case of the western frontier, the rights of the native inhabitants have largely been ignored and are in serious jeopardy. The federal government retains nominal ownership of most of the Alaskan lands, and monumental power struggles for possession are being fought between federal, state, and private interests. As in the case of Appalachia, the private developers are to a large extent absentee corporate giants.

But the most critical issue in the development of Alaska is the basic conflict which has characterized all recent U.S. regional development, namely the imposition of massive systems of technological exploitation upon a thin and fragile environment. Traditional U.S. assignment of highest priorities to use of technology to conquer nature in order to meet national and regional economic development goals poses a major threat to the future of one of the last major expanses of wilderness left in the nation.

The discovery of the new oil fields in Alaska and the rush to develop them have emphasized the harsh fact that neither at the federal level nor at the state level does there exist the planning and management capabilities essential to the development of these resources without irreversible damage to this vast region. The history of U.S. regional development, especially in Appalachia, offers critical lessons in the large scale mismanagement of resources systems, but it is questionable whether these lessons will be applied in time in Alaska to avoid repetition of the tragic Appalachian experience.

The major problem is that current technologies for the exploration, drilling, pumping, transportation, and refining of petroleum, based upon minimizing the private costs of exploitation, are among the most environmentally damaging of all technologies and impose enormous uncompensated social costs upon the regions in which they occur. Other factors adding to the vulnerability of the Alaskan environment create special problems. The delicate balance of nature characterized by the tundra and permafrost causes the normal practices of petroleum exploitation to result in unusually extensive and lasting damage to the environment. Waste products and litter generated on a vast scale by petroleum extraction in permafrost areas are not easily assimilated or recycled. Even minor disturbance of the permafrost cover for roads and facilities initiates processes of surface damage which nature cannot readily heal. Water drainage patterns are disrupted so that mud flats and water pollution are created.

Oil spills cause extensive damage to vegetation and wildlife over large areas of land and water. The areas being developed are subject to seismic activity which can cause breaks in pipelines which are difficult and costly to repair before extensive spillages have occurred. Both heat and cold add to the difficulty of preventing oil leaks. The arctic temperatures cause metal brittleness which adds to the probability of breaks. The elevated temperature of heated petroleum plus heat friction from pumping cause a tendency for the pipelines to sink into the tundra where breakages are likely and detection and repair are difficult. Oil spills and surface destruction pose a serious threat to the diminishing stocks of salmon, caribou, polar bears, arctic sheep, seals, walrus, whales, birds, and other wild life which provide the livelihood of the natives and which are of intrinsic value in the balance of nature.[1]

The initial success of the ice-breaking supertanker, Manhattan, in cutting through the ice of the Northwest Passage from Alaska to the ports of the eastern U.S. suggests that ocean transportation of oil may prove

1. For an excellent discussion of these problems, see Luther J. Carter, 1966.

feasible. However, the disastrous oil spills from the Torrey Canyon off the coast of England and the drilling operations off Santa Barbara in California offer early warnings of the associated dangers to ocean and shore resources from human failure and from the recurring probabilities of mechanical breakdowns.

The pressures for the accelerated development of the oil and other resources in Alaska are intensive. Development of additional domestic sources of supply is sought to replace depleted reserves and to reduce dependence upon foreign supplies. Oil leasing revenues and royalties have already provided nearly $1 billion in badly needed revenues to the government of Alaska. Production of large quantities of oil at low cost from the Alaskan reserves will generate large profits for some corporations and possible, but by no means assured, cost savings to consumers. However, the pressures to reduce private cost by shifting social costs to the environment through inadequate engineering of environmental safeguards may prove as costly to Alaska as the short run exploitation of resources in Appalachia by absentee owners.[2]

The evaluation of these benefits and costs will require more research efforts than have yet been devoted to the design of development planning and formulation of strategy for Alaska. State and federal planning capabilities are emerging, but no coherent overall regional development plan has been prepared. Despite the vast amounts of research and development expenditure by the oil companies, public sector planning has not prepared the necessary guidelines to protect the public interest in advance of the private development which is already underway. The legal rights of the Eskimos and Indians, as well as their future survival, is in severe jeopardy. Traditional U.S. priorities have placed development, technology and resource exploitation far in advance of the rights of minorities and the protection of the environment.

The issue in Alaska is whether the limited capabilities of an understaffed, provincial, isolated state government and a distant federal government with other competing priorities can respond adequately and in time to the enormous challenge of development already occurring in Alaska. History suggests that the institutions, mechanical technology, and political consensus necessary to develop the resources will emerge. Whether the response will be adequate to enhance the human values and protect

2. 'It can be argued that the oil industry had a sufficient interest in ensuring the integrity of the pipeline (and of the associated operations). However, it must be realized that the public has much more to lose than the industry, should a spill occur. The industry has so much to gain by getting the oil to market in an economical way that it may be worth the risks, whereas the dangers of a spill to the public may outweigh the benefits.' Daniel W. Swift, quoted in Carter, 1966.

the environmental and ecological resources in the region is a question which will provide a supreme challenge to the nation's regional development capabilities. The major challenge to federal and state development planners is to apply what has been observed in the history of U.S. regional development experience in order to guide the development pressures on Alaska into channels which serve general regional development, not merely economic development, and which can serve the human goals of all of the people of Alaska and the entire nation. However, these essential plans should be completed and implemented before, not after, development occurs. This is part of the larger challenge to economic development of finding improved methods of designing regional growth plans which will continue economic development without monumental and irreversible damage to the quality of environment and life.

The scale of research and planning currently devoted to Alaskan regional development appears to be inadequate in view of the magnitude of the problems and challenges. Numerous presidential commissions and interagency committees have been established. These include the Federal Field Program for Alaska, the Alaska Reconstruction and Development Commission, the Federal Field Committee for Development and Planning in Alaska, a Federal Advisory Council for Regional Economic Development and the President's Alaska Review Committee. However, what is urgently needed is an overall development strategy, identifying goals and priorities with analysis of the benefits and costs of alternative programs for achieving these objectives. A good case can be made that exploitation of the oil reserves should be postponed until such a plan can be completed, and that at least a modest fraction of the funds already obtained from the sale of oil leases should be allocated for this purpose. If only 5 percent of the funds obtained were reinvested to assure wise development of Alaskan resources, Alaska could establish a regional planning capability superior to that available in any other state. Such a modest investment in the future of the state would probably result in immediate and long-run benefits of many times this amount.

One possible method for achieving development without irreversible environmental damage would be to internalize the external diseconomies of resource allocation by requiring the oil companies and other developers to bear the full cost of preventing environmental pollution and of complete restoration of any damage that results directly or indirectly from their operations. If such requirements impose added costs on the developers, thereby reducing profits or increasing costs of the products, experience in other areas has indicated that the costs of good conservation practices can be borne by industry, if fairly and universally applied, without serious loss of profits or increase in the price of the final product.

Good conservation practice often results in increased efficiency of operations. However, even if profits are reduced and prices of Alaskan oil and other products must be increased, good resource allocation requires that these costs be borne by those who benefit from the industry rather than by the general public in terms of environmental damage.

CHAPTER XII

An empirical overview of the U.S. performance in regional economic development

Introduction

Preceding chapters have examined the wide range of regional development programs tested in the U.S. Although these programs have had numerous objectives, they have all shared the major goal of alleviating poverty. At this point it is useful to review the impact of U.S. regional development programs upon income levels.

By any general measures, the performance of the U.S. economy through its history in generating regional economic development has been impressive. Overall, steady economic growth has resulted in a high and rising level of real disposable per capita personal income for most of the residents in most of the regions of the nation. This is no small achievement, and its causes and consequences merit serious, detailed study. However, overall general averaging measurements conceal the variations in time, in space, and in composition which are the central concern in a study of regional development. Analysis of the regional and spatial dimensions of economic development is essential to a fuller understanding of the performance of the national economy over time.

The major thrusts in U.S. regional development since the winning of independence are readily summarized. Population growing rapidly from natural increase and from immigration spread extensively from the original Atlantic coast settlements across the nation to the Pacific. Early dependence upon primarily self-sufficient agrarian production evolved into a national market economy as investment in rapidly advancing transportation and in other technologies released labor from the farm, stimulating urban and industrial development. Individuals and groups which were able to raise their productivity through investment in human capital benefitted enormously from this process of economic growth, as did those regions characterized by a high percentage of high productivity residents. Individuals and groups less able to raise productivity and respond to changing opportunities participated to a lesser degree in the growing national productivity, as did those regions having high proportions of lower productivity residents.

The expansion in personal income

Reasonably reliable estimates of national and regional income have been constructed for the U.S. as far back as 1880.[1] At this time, the average per capita income, measured in dollar values of that period was approximately $186. However, regional differences were large. Per capita income was lowest in North Carolina ($64) in the Southeast region of the nation where regional incomes were lowest ($87). Personal per capita incomes were almost as low in the sparsely settled agricultural Southwest.

In contrast, incomes per capita in the New England, East, Great Lakes and the Plains regions, where more than half of the population lived, were much higher, reaching almost $300 in the wealthy states of Massachusetts and New York. The highest incomes in the nation are estimated to have been received in the Far West ($370) reaching the height of $606 in Nevada. However, this may be a statistical anomaly, resulting from the combination of very sparse population and very large mineral production. The same phenomena probably affected the high estimate for the Rocky Mountain States ($ 290).

By 1965 money incomes had risen more than fifteen-fold, reaching a nation average per capita of $2764. Interregional disparities were still great, being larger in absolute dollar amounts, but in relative terms, interstate differences in income levels had narrowed significantly, and the trend was towards national income equalization. Lowest per capita incomes were still found in the Southeast ($2103) being as low as $1615 in Mississippi. By a small margin, the Far West continued to be the region of highest per capita incomes ($3188). However, highest per capita incomes were found in the District of Columbia ($3694)[2] and in the state of Connecticut ($3455).

These income estimates are biased by many factors, including an increase in price levels of approximately 400 per cent during the 85 year period. Difficult index number problems and extensive changes in the composition of output raise serious questions about the validity of comparing income levels over a period characterized by such dynamic growth as this one. However, it is possible to make rough adjustments for price level changes in order to reduce some of the distortions in the figures.

1. Detailed tables on population, income, and unemployment are presented in the Appendix.
2. Treated in national statistics as a separate state.

In this case, the period 1957 to 1959 was used as a base period, and all income estimates were computed in terms of dollar values of that period. This procedure results in higher income estimates for the earlier period and lower estimates for the later period. However, the relative inter-regional differences remain constant, since no adjustment was made for differences in regional price levels.

On the basis of 1957-1959 price levels, the national average per capita personal income in the U.S. in 1965 was $2516. The lowest income levels in the nation were significantly below this being at less than $2000 in the Southeast, and were little more than half the national level in Mississippi ($1470). Low incomes persisted also in the Southwest ($2136) which were more than twice as high as those in the poorest states. Highest incomes were received in the District of Columbia ($3361) and in the State of Connecticut ($3144). High average personal incomes were also received in New England ($2754) and Mideast ($2843) and Great Lakes regions ($2740). Incomes in the Plains ($2409) and Rocky Mountain regions ($2322) were close to the national average.

Significance of the data

A number of important points should be noted about these income data. First, the basic data have been assembled from different sources, and are necessarily of different quality. The data from 1929 onward are drawn from detailed U.S. Department of Commerce statistics, and are highly reliable.[3] Income data for the period 1880-1920, though carefully constructed by experts in the field, are more conjectural (Kuznets, Thomas, Easterlin, 1960). The estimates of per capita income do not come from single consistent sources. Total income estimates from various sources have been divided by population estimates from other sources, and have been adjusted by price level figures in order to obtain adjusted per capita income estimates.

Also, the data, being from selected years, are not complete enough to reveal year to year fluctuations caused by cyclical and other factors. They do reveal the sharp decline associated with the Great Depression which affected the observations for 1930 and 1940, but otherwise they reveal steady secular growth and fail to identify short-run fluctuations. It should also be noted that the choice of geographical units (in this case,

3. It is relevant to note, however, that Oscar Morgenstern pointed out in a notable study, *On the Accuracy of Economic Observations* (Princeton University Press, 1950), that even official GNP estimates may contain errors of about 10 per cent, with much larger errors in some of the individual income components which are more difficult to measure.

states) affects the figures. States are seldom homogeneous socio-economic units, and they conceal intraregional variation. The smaller the type of region chosen, the greater the amount of interregional variation to be expected. This regional unit was accepted as the unit of measurement because data are more readily available in this form over longer periods than for other units, such as counties and metropolitan areas.

Some factors related to regional income differentials

Numerous factors affect the differences in per capita income observed in different regions. Historically in the U.S. higher incomes have been positively associated with higher levels of education, high percentages of work force in industrial employment, low levels of unemployment, high labor force participation ratios, high percentage of white population, high percentage of population in urban areas, favorable resource endowment, extensive capital accumulation, and related factors. In general, these are factors which appear to have acted favorably in raising productivity and income. Conversely, lower per capita incomes are associated with lower work force participation ratios, high percentage of population in rural areas, high percentage of non-white populations, poor resource endowment, and lower investment in human and in physical capital. In many occupations, women are paid less than men, and families with women as the head tend to have incomes lower than families headed by men.

Table 4 shows differentials over time between the income levels of white and non-white families and individuals. In 1939, the median annual income levels of whites was $1325 as compared with only 37 percent of this figure, $489, for non-white families. However, there was constant improvement in both the absolute and relative level of median incomes for non-whites which rose by 1955 to 55 percent of that for white families. In the next decade by 1965, median incomes for non-white families had risen to $3,994, though this was still only 55 percent of the median income level for white families and individuals.

Table 4. *Median income of families and individuals, white and non-white*

Families and individuals	1939	1947	1950	1955	1960	1965
White, median income	1,325	3,157	3,445	4,605	5,835	7,251
Non-white, median income	489	1,614	1,869	2,549	3,233	3,994
Non-white as a percent of white	36.9	51.1	54.3	55.4	55.4	55.1

Source: U.S. Department of Commerce, Bureau of the Census, Current Population Reports, Series P. 60.

Table 5. *Percent distribution of families, by income level, by years of school completed, and color of head, 1966*

	Elementary School		High School		College	
Color of head and income level	Less than 8 years	8 years	1 to 3 years	4 years	1 to 3 years	4 years or more
WHITE FAMILIES (in thousands)	4,911	7,114	7,853	13,717	4,665	5,757
Percent	100.0	100.0	100.0	100.0	100.0	100.0
Income under 3,000	33.1	19.9	11.9	7.2	6.1	4.3
3,000 to 4,999	21.7	18.6	14.6	10.6	7.5	5.2
5,000 to 6,999	18.4	21.1	20.6	18.9	14.9	9.2
7,000 to 9,999	16.5	22.2	27.4	29.9	28.3	20.6
10,000 to 14,999	7.5	14.2	20.1	24.9	28.6	31.9
15,000 and over	2.7	4.0	5.4	8.4	14.6	28.9
Median income in $	4,477	6,103	7,267	8,217	9,252	11,697
NON-WHITE FAMILIES						
(in thousands)	1,551	678	1,133	1,023	285	235
Percent	100.00	100.00	100.0	100.0	100.0	100.0
Income under 3,000	45.2	31.9	29.8	18.1	11.0	7.6
3,000 to 4,999	26.1	26.0	27.4	21.7	16.2	5.5
5,000 to 6,999	14.4	15.8	16.8	21.3	22.5	13.6
7,000 to 9,999	9.6	18.3	15.9	21.2	27.5	28.5
10,000 to 14,999	3.9	6.9	7.6	14.4	21.1	29
15,000 and over	0.9	1.0	2.6	3.4	1.8	15.3
Median income in $	3,349	4,399	4,418	5,886	7.043	9,510
Non-white median income as a percent of white	74.8	72.1	60.8	71.6	76.1	81.3

Source: U.S. Department of Commerce, Bureau of the Census, Current Population Report, Series P-60, No. 53.

Income levels of families are highly correlated with the level of education. The columns in Table 5 show that the percentages of families in high income categories rise sharply with the number of years education of the head of the family and that the reverse is true for the low income categories. For those in white families with less than 8 years of education, median incomes in 1966 were $4,447, but for those whose head had 4 or more years of higher education, median family income was $11,697.

Unfortunately, education alone has not been sufficient to eliminate the differences in income levels between white and non-white families, though

Table 6. *Unemployed persons, age 18 and over by color and years of school completed*

Years of school completed and color	1968 Unemployed	Rate	1966 Unemployed	Rate	1964 Unemployed	Rate	1962 Unemployed	Rate
ALL PERSONS								
Total: Number (thousands)	2576	3.4	2646	3.7	3861	5.5	4049	6.0
Per cent	100.0	—	100.0	—	100.0	—	100.0	—
Elementary: 8 years or less	25.0	4.4	30.0	5.0	33.8	7.6	36.1	8.0
High School: 1 to 3 years	28.7	5.4	27.1	5.3	25.2	7.3	26.8	8.3
4 years of High School or more	46.2	2.6	43.0	2.7	41.0	4.0	37.0	4.1
4 years	33.5	3.1	30.7	3.1	29.7	4.8	27.7	5.1
1 years of College or more	12.8	1.8	12.3	2.0	11.3	2.9	9.3	2.6
Median school years completed	11.6	—	11.2	—	10.9	—	10.6	—
WHITE								
Total: Number (in thousands)	2033	3.0	2084	3.3	3092	5.0	3138	2.5
Per cent	100.0	—	100.0	—	100.0	—	100.0	—
Elementary: 8 years or more	24.4	4.1	28.9	4.7	32.7	7.2	33.9	7.1
High School: 1 to 3 years	26.6	4.6	25.4	4.5	23.7	6.4	26.1	7.2
4 years of High School or more	49.0	2.3	45.7	2.4	43.6	3.7	40.0	3.7
4 years	34.5	2.7	32.3	2.8	31.5	4.3	29.5	4.6
1 year of College or more	14.5	1.7	13.4	1.8	12.1	2.6	10.5	2.4
Median school years completed	11.9	—	11.5	—	11.2	—	10.9	—
NON-WHITE								
Total: Number (in thousands)	543	6.5	562	7.0	769	10.0	911	12.1
Per cent	100	—	100.0	—	100.0	—	100.0	—
Elementary: 8 years or more	27.4	5.4	33.8	6.3	38.4	9.4	43.8	11.7
High School: 1 to 3 years	36.8	9.8	33.6	9.7	31.1	12.5	29.4	15.3
4 years of High School or more	35.7	5.4	32.7	6.1	30.6	8.8	26.8	10.3
4 years	29.5	6.7	24.7	7.0	22.5	10.1	21.5	12.4
1 year of College or more	6.3	2.8	8.0	4.3	8.1	6.5	5.3	6.1
Median school years completed	10.8	—	10.5	—	10.1	—	9.6	—

Source: Elizabeth Waldman, 'Educational attainment of workers'. *Monthly Labor Review* (U.S. Department of Labor) Vol. 92 (2), 1969.

for non-white families, the same strong positive correlation is present between income levels and years of education. For non-white families those with heads having less than 8 years of education had median income in 1966 of $3,349, as compared with $9,510 for those whose heads had 4 or more years of college. For every level of education incomes for whites were higher than those for non-whites. The reasons for this unfortunate phenomenon are multiple and complex, including prejudice and the fact that the quality of education available to non-whites has not been comparable to that available to whites.

Race and educational level in the U.S. strongly affect unemployment rates as well as income levels. Unemployment rates of course, vary cyclically and seasonally with the general performance of the economy. However, despite the general level of prosperity, non-whites suffer from a higher level of unemployment, though the rate of unemployment declines as the number of years of education increases. Table 6 shows that while in 1968 the rate of unemployment for whites was 3.0 percent, that for non-whites overall was 6.5 percent. Unemployment rates for both groups were highest for those completing 1 to 3 years of high school, with 4.6 percent unemployed in the white group and almost 10 percent of non-whites in this important group.

Despite these inequities, it should be noted that the general level of income for non-whites has approached approximately three-quarters of the income level for whites, and many non-white families receive incomes which would be regarded as affluent throughout most of the world (Friedmann, 1966). However, the remaining incidence of poverty has become increasingly visible, and vigorous anti-poverty efforts have been made in recent years in order to identify and ameliorate the causes of poverty.

Evaluation

Ultimately, concern with the regional divergence of levels of economic activity results from concern for its impact upon the residents in these regions. This brief survey has indicated that the overall performance of the U.S. economy has been distinctly impressive in generating high and rising levels of personal income throughout the nation. However, this excellent performance has been marred by the persistence of poverty in some states and some regions and among many groups and individuals. The highly developed market economy of the U.S. offers large incomes to those whose productivity, mobility, and motivation have permitted them to function effectively in this economy. However, large numbers have remained impoverished and have not participated fully in the American

Table 7. *Incidence of poverty in the total population and the distribution of the poor*

Characteristics	Incidence of poverty, 1966 (per cent poor in each group)	Distribution of persons living below the poverty level			
		1959		1966	
		Number (millions)	Per-cent	Number (millions)	Per-cent
Total	15	39	100	30	100
COLOR					
White	12	28	72	20	67
Non-white	41	11	28	9	32
LOCATION*					
Central cities of SMSA's**	16	—	—	9	32
Outside central citis of SMSA's	9	—	—	6	19
Small cities, towns and rural	21	—	—	15	49
AGE AND FAMILY HEAD					
Persons 65 years and over	30	6	15	5	17
Children under 18	18	17	43	13	42
In families with male head	13	13	33	8	27
In families with female head	61	4	10	5	15
All persons in households with female head	42	11	27	11	36

* Information not available for 1959.
** Standard Metropolitan Statistical Areas.

Source: Social Security Bulletin, *Annual Statistical Supplement, 1966*, Table 8, p. 6 and *idem*, March 1968, Mollie Orshansky, 'The Shape of Poverty in 1966,' Table 3, 4, 7 and 8, pp. 6, 7, 14 and 17.

economy, primarily because of low productivity resulting from inadequate education, racial prejudice, poor health, excessive family size, immobility, cultural barriers, and related problems which in many cases have cumulative effects from generation to generation. Unfortunately, these factors have affected some groups more consistently than others, such as Negroes, Indians and Puerto Ricans. There remain extensive pockets of poverty both in urban and rural areas among whites and non-whites. As a percentage of total U.S. population, the numbers existing in extreme poverty (as defined below) is small, at most 15 per cent, but this is a much

Table 8. *Annual earnings of 4-quarter wage and salary workers, 1966*

Major industry in 1964	Median annual earnings (in $)
Lumber and wood products, except furniture	4,122
Furniture and fixtures	4,435
Apparel and other finished products	2,889
Leather and leather products	3,430
Retail trade	2,937
Automotive dealers and gasoline and service stations	4,706
Gasoline and service stations	3,572
Apparel and accessory stores	2,917
Furniture, home furnishings and equipment stores	4,567
Eating and drinking places	2,147
Banking	4,353
Hotels, rooming houses, camps, other lodging	2,496
Laundries, laundry services, cleaning, dyeing	2,729
Auto repair, services, garages	4,649
Medical and other health services	3,156
Private household	1,061

* Table from p. 35 of Perspectives on Poverty, *op. cit.*

larger relative and absolute part of the total population in poverty than is acceptable in affluent industrial society.

Given the poverty level as defined by the U.S. Social Security Administration (about $3,300 for a nonfarm family of four in 1966), Table 7 shows that the number affected by poverty in the U.S. fell from 39 million in 1954 to 30 million in 1966. By 1966, the number of non-whites affected by poverty had fallen to 9 million but this represented a disproportionately large percentage of the non-white group. Most of the poor lived outside the central cities of metropolitan areas, and poverty is greatest among the most dependent age groups (the young and the aged) and among those who encounter the most economic and social discrimination (D. K. Newman, 1969). Incomes are also significantly affected by industry of occupation. Table 8, which is based upon a sample including all earnings regardless of primary source, cites average 1966 earnings for some low paying industries. All of these factors contribute to the high levels of interregional income variance in the U.S.

Despite well known and serious problems in international comparison of income variance some approximate orders of magnitude can be shown. Table 9 shows per capita income in the U.S. for 1965 ($2,893). Table 10

Table 9. *Per capita national income in selected countries, 1965*

Country	Per capita national income (In U.S. $)
United States	2,893
Argentina	740
Australia	1,620
Brazil	217
Canada	1,825
Chile	515
France	1,436
West Germany	1,447
Israel	1,067
Italy	883
Japan	696
Korea	88
Mexico	412
Netherlands	1,265
Nigeria	63
South Africa	509
Switzerland	1,928
United Kingdom	1,451
Venezuela	745
Viet Nam	113

Source: United Nations Monthly Bulletin of Statistics, October, 1967, pp. xx-xxii quoted in Chandler, 1969.

Table 10. *International comparisons of per capita income*

	Per capita income (In U.S. $)	
	High province	Low province
Belgium	1,231	801
Denmark	1,481	972
France	2,019	532
Germany	1,550	606
Italy	944	272
Netherlands	1,143	731
Sweden	1,848	987
United Kingdom	1,887	539
United States family income, 1959:		
Tunica County (Miss.)	—	1,260
Owsley County (Ky.)	—	1,324
Montgomery County (Md.)	9,317	—

Source: Chandler, 1969, p. 55.

shows that per capita incomes ranged from a high of $9,317 in wealthy Montgomery County, Maryland to a low of $1,260 in Tunica County in bottom-ranking Mississippi, and $1,324 in the Appalachian County of Owsley in Kentucky. However, it is important to note in Table 10 that residents in these lowest per capita income counties in the U.S. had much higher per capita incomes than those in the low income provinces of Western Europe and indeed higher incomes than in some of the high income provinces in Western Europe.

There has been intensive continuing concern about the extent of poverty in the U.S. especially since the Great Depression of the 1930's, when the President, Franklin D. Roosevelt, noted that one-third of the nation existed in poverty. Despite progress in alleviating poverty in absolute terms, rising levels of affluence in the general economy have properly served to focus more attention on the hard core of poverty which remains. Consequently, in recent years more intensive research on the causes of poverty have led to imaginatively bold new programs, and proposals such as the guaranteed annual wage, and the negative income tax (Aaron, 1969). This same concern with poverty, especially where it is widespread and concentrated throughout entire regions, such as Appalachia, has been a major factor in the design and implementation of the recent federal regional development programs examined in this study. The limited success of regional development programs in alleviating poverty and in achieving the other objectives indicates an urgent need to evaluate past regional development efforts and identify opportunities for future improvement.

CHAPTER XIII

The future of regional development

Introduction: The quality of the performance

Regional and urban development represents the spatial disaggregation of national economic development policies as these policies directly affect people and their lives. The importance of regional development emerges from the fact that it determines in large measure how economic policy permeates the quality of life. In the U.S., regional development policy, in reflecting national values and culture, has achieved notable successes, but successes which have been purchased at very high cost. The successes and benefits of U.S. regional development experience can be measured in terms of high and rising per capita levels of real income for a large majority of the population. The number and percent of the U.S. population living below poverty levels is falling.

However, the most notable failure of U.S. regional development policy is the fact that despite the general affluence the percentage of the population still remaining below the poverty level (approximately 25 percent) is unacceptably high, both as a national average and in its higher concentration in many regions, in urban ghettos, among racial minorities, and among other disadvantaged groups. Another major shortcoming of U.S. regional development policies is that the high average level of development which has been achieved has been bought at the cost of air and water pollution, resource mismanagement, urban decay, debasement of the countryside, and widespread environmental deterioration.

The major tasks of regional development in the U.S. for the future are therefore to find improved methods for extending the benefits of economic development to impoverished groups and to find improved methods of economic development which result in less deterioration of urban areas, less destruction of the general environment, and less damage to the quality of life. Increasing alienation of various groups and the growing dissatisfaction of the young during a period of unprecedented economic growth suggest that mere continued acceleration of aggregative growth is not sufficient, but that what is now needed is drastic improvement in the qualitative aspects of regional and urban development.

Some sources of success and failure

A partial explanation for both the impressive achievements of U.S. regional development policy and for its serious failures can be found in the basic values, beliefs, and goals of U.S. society, which have shaped its national and regional development policy. The emphasis upon political freedom and equality of opportunity to pursue individual objectives, including economic advancement, was extended to belief in the right of each region to compete for maximum economic growth. Interregional competition for specialization and growth contributed to the rapid development of an efficient national market economy. A pragmatic, pluralistic, open approach to the design of institutions and government programs was valuable both in assuring that most of the groups affected by development programs could participate in the planning process and in gaining political acceptance for regional development programs. These are all values which have served the nation well in achieving its economic aspirations, and which will be necessary ingredients in improving future efforts.

Some of the other basic values in shaping U.S. regional development efforts, useful though they may have been in the past, are in need of re-appraisal in the light of changing events and changing priorities. One of the basic values which is being increasingly questioned is the belief in the unlimited rights of individuals, firms, and regions to exploit natural resources, land, and environmental factors for short-run profit with inadequate concern for long-run management policy and without protecting the total environmental system. The tragic mismanagement of natural resources and the exploitation of the human resources of Appalachia is an example of failure to recognize the interrelationships between human and natural resource systems and the need for long-run total systems planning for regional development.

In earlier periods of U.S. history when a small population with primitive technologies faced the task of occupying and subduing a hostile environment, the belief in man's right to conquer nature and bend the environment to his will was an appropriate and necessary belief. But today with high population densities spread across the continent, applying ever more powerful technologies to relatively shrinking reserves of space and resources, the belief in limitless options for human modification of the biosphere is in need of re-appraisal in the light of modern knowledge of ecology and environmental management. Accumulating evidence of widespread general deterioration in environmental quality suggests the need for more sophisticated and cautious approaches to the management of natural and environmental resources.

Another basic value which has contributed to the growth and productivity of the nation and its regions has been supreme confidence in technological change, and the willingness to accept and adapt to the implications of the total systems change that accompanies new technologies especially in the evaluation of transportation, communications, and energy production. The willingness of U.S. society to accept change, to identify it as progress, and to adapt to its systems requirements has been especially notable in the transition from canals to railroads and to the automobile. While this ready acceptance of extensive new technologies has undoubtedly contributed to the pace of economic development, it has become increasingly evident that some new technologies, though having great potential for regional development, may carry with them the seeds of potential disaster. It is becoming recognized that new technologies, especially on a large scale, are seldom unmixed blessings, and their indirect, long-run effects need careful study and regulation. The effects of extensive automobile transportation on urban air quality is one example. The growing concern over the ecological effects of DDT and other agricultural chemicals is another example. Development of supersonic transport aircraft poses the threat of widespread sonic booming and further deterioration in the quality of life.

The releases of radioactivity into the environment from the mining, processing, transportation, and use of nuclear materials is probably the most serious potential threat to environmental safety from the introduction of new systems of technology. While all of these technologies can potentially contribute much to regional and national economic development if properly planned and controlled, the possibilities of widespread and perhaps irreversible damage from them suggest that uncritical confidence in the benefits of advanced technology is a traditional value which is urgently in need of re-evaluation. Technology is a powerful extension of human capabilities and can be used constructively or destructively. More sophistication and caution is needed in the assessment of the costs as well as of the benefits and of the indirect as well as of the direct effects of new technologies upon regional development.

Another basic value which has contributed positively, as noted above, to U.S. regional development has been the belief in the inalienable right of every region to compete for maximum attainable growth. The strength of this belief is so well established in U.S. regional development thinking that it is seldom questioned. However valuable though this force has been historically in achieving high levels of national and regional economic activity, it is becoming increasingly apparent that although all regions should have equal opportunity to compete for growth, it is not necessarily in the interest of the nation or of its regions to encourage or require all regions to compete for growth. It is also extremely important to reconsider the ground rules for interregional competition for growth in order to improve the balance between regional and national economic development goals.

In many ways, regions today are forced to compete for growth, whether they wish to or not, especially by placing major responsibility to finance public sector services upon local government. The result has been pressures for excessive growth in some areas, as evidenced by exhaustion of local water supplies and massive water transfers, overloading of waste removal facilities, urban congestion, breakdown of transportation facilities, and in the intensive settlement of areas unsuitable for development because of periodic drought, brush fires, flooding, seismic activity, earth slides, and other natural phenomena.

All of these problems suggest that even in view of the impressive achievements of U.S. regional development programs, possible opportunities for improvement exist.

On the possibilities for improved performance

The appraisal of these successes and failures of U.S. regional development experience leads naturally to the question of how future performance in this important field can be improved.

A first step in improving the U.S. performance in regional development would be to establish what has been conspicuously lacking since the early federal period, namely a conscious, positive policy for regional development based upon a revised set of goals and priorities relevant to the values of contemporary society. The history of the U.S. experience to date provides affirmative reasons for believing that once a conscious set of positive goals for regional development has been identified by traditional processes of consensus, an efficient strategy and set of programs can be designed to achieve the goals which are sought. The history of U.S. experience also suggests some of the elements which might be incorporated into an improved set of policies, programs and strategies for regional development.

A first characteristic of a successful U.S. policy for regional development is that it must be a truly federal program, based upon full recognition of the federal, state and local governments as well as of private interests. The appropriate role of the federal government is to provide leadership in analysis of the problem, identify a consensus concerning goals, design the general guidelines to be followed, establish rules of the game which ensure that interregional competition serves the general interest, evaluate the issues raised in considering alternative programs, support the research necessary to resolve these issues, provide the technical assistance needed by local governments in carrying out programs, coordinate the activities of federal, state and local agencies, and continually monitor and improve the resulting programs.

This is a much more comprehensive role for the federal government than it has traditionally followed in regional development, which has generally been limited to the disbursement of funds through the existing establishment. Analysis of the past suggests that the time has come for this historic federal role of distributing funds for the unselective encouragement of universal regional growth to give way to a more selective policy concerned with improving the quality of regional growth by explicit recognition of spatial relationships, resource management objectives and by the requirements for environmental protection. It has become clear that some restrictions on uncontrolled regional development are essential in the larger public interest if the nation is to protect and manage its water resources, wilderness areas, recreational sites, and the quality of its environment.

Although the political difficulties of doing so might be serious, a major contribution to the improvement of regional development practice in the U.S. would be for the federal government, with the concurrence of the states and localities, to evolve a specific national policy on regional development which would determine not only general policy on spatial distribution of economic activity as between rural, suburban and urban regions, but which would also identify those areas for which the national interest was best served by limiting growth, and those areas which should be encouraged to grow.

Federal guidelines are also necessary and desirable in order to avoid forcing states and regions to engage in competitive deterioration of resource management in the unrestrained contest for accelerated growth. Federal regulations and guidelines are essential in protecting environmental resources, in setting aside wilderness reserves, and in regulating the intensity of regional development in areas having a high probability of disastrous losses of human life and property damage because of periodic floodings, shore erosion, seismic activity, landslides, brushfires, and disastrous weather phenomena. Stronger federal initatives are also necessary in the coordination of development-related federal, state, and local programs for which sub-national jurisdictions are sub-optimal in size, such as those affecting transportation systems, river basins, electric power networks, communication systems, natural resource systems and environmental management. These policy areas are inseparable from regional development, and must be addressed simultaneously.

The conduct of a more activist role by the federal government in regional planning will encounter the traditional widespread and well-established reluctance to permit federal agencies to engage in specific, programmed, detailed spatial planning. However, realistic examination of actual practice indicates that the federal government already directly determines the location of a large proportion of all economic activity in the nation through its own programs of capital construction expenditures and operations. It further affects the location of more of the nation's total economic activity through its regulatory powers and federal relationships with local governments. Furthermore, the federal government still owns significant amounts of land outright, especially in the West. Consequently, the federal government cannot be neutral in its effects upon regional development, and since it does directly, indirectly, or potentially control the spatial configuration of regional activity, the necessity for a conscious and positive federal policy for regional development grows more compelling and inescapable.

An important factor in implementing a federal policy for regional development would be the requirement that state, regional, and local governments refer their regional plans for development to the federal level for approval in order to assure consistency with plans of other regions and with national guidelines. However, even with a positive national policy for regional development, it is clear that state, regional, and local governments would have major roles to play as they have had traditionally. Most of the detailed physical planning and programming would necessarily be accomplished at the local levels, which now have responsibility for planning and zoning. However, just as it appears necessary for the federal government to play a more active future role in establishing both broad guidelines and specific plans for systems such as those for resource management having extensive external effects, so state governments will probably find it necessary to provide more leadership in physical planning and resource management than they have in the past in order to coordinate sub-state programs.

As state and local governments aspire to upgrade their regional planning efforts, one of the most important advancements needed is the replacement of narrow promotional economic development planning with more general planning for the overall social development of the region emphasizing improvement of regional productivity, improvement by local government of public sector services, protection of environmental quality, and improvement of the quality of life in the region.

Success in such efforts will require the evolution of traditional economic development agencies into general regional development agencies reflecting the broader aspirations of the entire community, of which the business community is but one part.

An important element in a federal structure for regional development is the role of interregional competition for economic growth. It has been observed that traditional policies of leaving the responsibility for financing public services to the local government impose pressures upon every region to pursue high rates of economic growth. If the nation and the states are to become more selective in the identification of regions for more intensive growth and regions for less intensive growth, a necessary accompaniment of this policy is more revenue sharing from federal to state governments, and likewise from state to local governments. If revenue sharing were encouraged especially for programs of education, health, and training, reduction of poverty and other forms of investment in human capital, this policy would have the multiple advantage of reducing disparities in levels of economic development, making migration from depressed areas more feasible, and improving the quality of life for those who preferred to remain in lagging regions.

Another important element in improving the quality of regional development would be to adopt federal guidelines which encourage regions to compete for development in other ways which increase the productivity of regions and their residents rather than competing for growth by offering local tax concessions and other subsidies which do not necessarily raise regional or national productivity. Interregional competition for growth by adopting programs to improve local productivity through investment in human resources, enhancement of local amenities, and raising the general quality of life and environment could benefit both the region and the nation. Such programs could go far to reconcile conflicts between regional and national development goals.

In order that the federal government may play a more positive and constructive role for providing leadership and guidelines for U.S. regional development, it will be essential to adopt new programs of planning, research, coordination, and administration. Among the most important new national programs required for the improvement of regional development in the U.S. is a comprehensive program for management of the natural resources and the protection of environmental resources. The need for fundamental improvement in resource management is underlined historically by the problems that poor resource practices of the past have left in Appalachia, and by the growing threat of such problems as the oil spills resulting from drilling operations off the California coast near Santa Barbara. As the nation embarks upon larger programs for exploitation of oil in Alaska, oil shale deposits in the West, and of the resources of the oceans, the need for more sophisticated systems of planning and management becomes more apparent.

One concept which is needed in programs for the management of resource systems is the concept of life cycle planning, which involves comprehensive forward planning of resource management through all phases of exploitation, development, extraction, transportation, and eventual restoration. This concept applied to strip mining, for example, would require that resource developers, before beginning any operations, would be required to produce responsible, comprehensive plans to show that they had programmed the exploration, extraction, transportation, and processing of resources, with eventual restoration of the resource system without irreversible damage to water, air, or land at any stage of operations. This type of requirement might or might not raise costs of extracting and selling resource products. If costs and prices were increased, the full social costs of production including environmental protection should be borne by the producers and consumers of the resources. Otherwise, the resources should not be developed until such time as private costs are made to reflect full social costs. Vigorous application of this approach to resource management at the federal level would correct many of the current abuses in regional development and go far to improve the quality of both national and regional development.

Another important concept which could provide significant guidelines for national planning of regional development, especially in determining the role of technology, is the concept of environmental neutrality of technology. Currently, pressures of interregional and interfirm competition provide incentives for the premature adoption of technologies which appear to yield short-run economic gains at the cost of long-run environmental damage. Examples are the hasty and inadequately researched introduction of DDT and other agricultural chemicals, nuclear energy, the supersonic transport plane and other technologies which cause pollution, thermal waste, radioactivity, noise and other forms of environmental deterioration. Yet these technologies have many potential benefits for humanity, provided that they can be sufficiently perfected in advance of application to eliminate their dangers. However, in order to determine their safety in advance of introduction, highly qualified panels of physical, social, and behavioral scientists would have to be given the opportunity to evaluate the total systems implications of these technologies and judge their probable impact upon society resulting from the total system needed to support the technology in question. As resource systems such as nuclear power and agricultural chemicals become more extensive and powerful, they cease to become matters of mere regional or even national concern, but can potentially affect the entire biosphere of the globe. Increasingly, national and international efforts will be needed to assess the environmental and total systems implications of new technologies before widespread introduction is approved or permitted.

Regional development policies are so linked with other socio-economic problems that they can not be solved in isolation. The need to design an overall national policy for regional development is becoming apparent, but it is equally apparent that performing this task will require the concurrent design of consistent national policies on the related issues of urban development, transportation planning, technology assessment, population management, land use, resource management, and environmental protection.

It would be misleading to suggest that all of the essential information for improved regional development is available and that all of the critical questions have been answered. Important gaps remain in theory, information, and in understanding. The most critical element of regional development planning is continued research and analysis. The most important single program element in regional development policy is continuous research, evaluation and reappraisal of theories, goals, issues, and alternative approaches to the problem.[1]

Major gaps in regional development theory still remain. Much more information is needed on the economies of scale and interspatial relationships between hierarchies of city size. This information is essential in order to develop realistic national policies on city size and location, the role of new towns, and optimal balance between urban, suburban and rural settlement. More information is needed on interregional flows of goods, services, transactions, commuting and other activities. Research is needed on the environmental and ecological impacts of different types and patterns of economic activity. A fundamental problem underlying regional development is the problem of rapid population growth. High rates of population expansion aggravate all problems of regional development, as well as all other basic economic and social problems. Major research efforts are necessary for understanding the nature of the population problem, and for finding generally acceptable methods for dealing with this fundamental force. Information is needed on factors affecting migration and the regional demand and supply functions of factors of production. More data are needed on the interregional spatial linkages between economic and other activities. There is urgent need for the extension of traditional location theory dealing with market activity to problems of location criteria in the public sector. Although the U.S.

1. For a list of research priorities, see Appendix B, suggested list.

economy and its regions are highly adaptable to changes in demand, supply, technology, and policy relationships, sudden large changes can cause distress in some economic activities in some regions. Although large-scale federal expenditures on extensive technological systems, such as weapons, space, and supersonic transport systems generate exhilarating regional prosperity when expanding their reduction can bring widespread regional distress and resistance to policy change. The design of improved programs for aiding regional economic readjustment and for alleviating distress is vital not only for humanitarian reasons but in order to prevent distortion of national interests and policy decisions by disproportionate and unnecessary local pressures.

Most importantly, research is needed on the relationships between different types and patterns of economic activity and broader aspects of general regional social development. New systems of regional social accounts and social indicators (Olsen, 1969) will be essential if regional and urban economic development programs are to be made more responsive to the achievement of contemporary human goals.

Summary

In the history of the U.S. experience in regional development, there has been a continuing tendency for the federal government to play a central, though far from an exclusive role, in determining policies and programs. The consistent logic behind this federal role has been the fact that regional development both requires and generates external economies and diseconomies. When the spatial distribution of these externalities extends beyond the geographic boundaries of the decision-making units involved, the possibility emerges for a higher level of decision-making to reduce the degree of suboptimisation, and improve resource allocation processes.

During the era of internal improvements, Gallatin and others perceived that while transportation systems were a prerequisite to economic development of the nation's resources and its regions, adequate investment in transportation was unlikely to be undertaken either by private investors or local governments, because they would be unable to capture all of the profits. Spill-over benefits would accrue over regions beyond the control of local agencies. Under these circumstances, the amount of investment made in transportation would be sub-optimal unless the federal government developed a national plan and provided financial subsidies, as it decided to do. This same logic was followed more or less successfully in the case of state and local subsidies for local systems. To the extent that these systems were well-designed with respect to relationships between urban centers, resource supply areas, market areas, and transport linkages, and were efficiently implemented, they resulted in major advances in regional development.

However, in more recent times, external diseconomies of economic development have become increasingly recognized as causing requirements for federal intervention of a different nature. Large scale external diseconomies resulting from pollution, congestion, and environmental deterioration have been intensified, and accelerated urban and regional development are generating wastes and residuals which producers and consumers discharge into common property resources of air and water. The divergence between private cost and social cost is resulting in excessive exploitation of resources and waste of output in those industries and activities which do not bear the full social cost of proper waste management. The U.S. is now faced with the urgent need to design national, regional, and urban development programs which can generate the growing production needed to meet urgent social priorities while restoring and protecting the quality of life and environment. This will not be an easy task, but it is one which will require at least as much imagination, innovation, and effort which was devoted to earlier programs for economic development.

Finally, regional economic development in the U.S., despite its major successes, and despite efforts to justify it on the basis of poverty alleviation, has benefited primarily the affluent and the established, leaving behind too many victims of discrimination, members of minority groups, alienated sub-cultures, and young persons who assign social justice, human values, and the quality of life priority over economic development. The major future challenge of regional and urban development will be to relate economic development more effectively to improvements in the quality of life for man in his total environment.

APPENDIX A

Statistical sources

Table A-1. *Population of the United States, 1790-1965* (in thousands)

States and Regions	1790	1800	1810	1820	1830	1840	1850	1860	1870
New England	1009	1233	1472	1660	1955	2235	2728	3135	3488
Maine	97	152	229	298	399	502	583	628	627
New Hampshire	142	184	214	244	269	285	318	326	318
Vermont	85	154	218	236	281	292	314	315	331
Massachusetts	379	423	472	523	610	738	995	1231	1457
Rhode Island	69	69	77	83	97	109	148	175	217
Connecticut	238	251	262	275	298	310	371	460	537
Mideast	1337	1816	2483	3203	4142	5108	6626	8333	9849
New York	340	589	959	1373	1919	2429	3097	3881	4383
New Jersey	184	211	246	278	321	373	490	672	906
Pennsylvania	434	602	810	1049	1348	1724	2312	2906	3522
Delaware	59	64	73	73	77	78	92	112	125
Maryland	320	342	381	407	447	470	583	687	781
District of Columbia	—	8	15	23	30	34	52	75	132
Great Lakes	—	51	272	793	1470	2925	4523	6927	9125
Michigan	—	—	5	9	32	212	398	749	1184
Ohio	—	45	231	581	938	1519	1980	2340	2665
Indiana	—	6	25	147	343	686	988	1350	1681
Illinois	—	—	12	55	157	476	851	1712	2540
Wisconsin	—	—	—	—	—	31	305	776	1055
Plains	—	—	20	67	140	427	880	2170	3857
Minnesota	—	—	—	—	—	—	6	172	440
Iowa	—	—	—	—	—	43	192	675	1194
Missouri	—	—	20	67	140	384	682	1182	1721
North Dakota	—	—	—	—	—	—	—	5	2
South Dakota	—	—	—	—	—	—	—	—	12
Nebraska	—	—	—	—	—	—	—	29	123
Kansas	—	—	—	—	—	—	—	107	364
Southeast	1584	2210	2993	3915	5155	6368	8044	9655	10,432
Virginia	692	808	878	938	1044	1025	1119	1220	1225
West Virginia	56	79	105	137	177	225	302	377	442
Kentucky	74	221	407	564	688	708	982	1156	1321
Tennessee	36	106	262	423	682	829	1003	1110	1259
North Carolina	394	478	556	639	738	753	869	993	1071
South Carolina	249	346	415	503	581	594	669	704	706
Georgia	83	163	252	341	517	691	906	1057	1184
Florida	—	—	—	—	35	54	87	140	188
Alabama	—	1	9	128	310	591	772	964	997
Mississippi	—	8	31	75	137	376	607	791	828
Louisiana	—	—	77	153	216	352	518	708	727
Arkansas	—	—	1	14	30	98	210	435	484

1880	1890	1900	1910	1920	1929	1930	1940	1950	1960	1965
4011	4701	5592	6553	7401	8130	8166	8437	9314	10,527	11,151
649	661	694	742	768	797	797	847	914	974	985
347	377	412	431	443	467	465	492	533	609	673
332	332	344	356	352	359	360	359	378	389	403
1783	2239	2805	3366	3852	4229	4250	4317	4691	5154	5361
277	346	429	543	604	684	687	713	792	858	891
623	746	908	1115	1381	1594	1607	1709	2007	2543	2838
11,757	14,146	17,107	21,144	24,372	28,223	28,617	30,290	33,626	38,613	41,325
5083	6003	7269	9114	10,385	12,171	12,588	13,479	14,830	16,855	18,107
1131	1445	1884	2537	3156	3989	4041	4160	4835	6104	6793
4283	5258	6302	7665	8720	9723	9631	9900	10,498	11,328	11,587
147	168	185	202	223	236	238	267	318	449	505
935	1042	1188	1295	1450	1621	1632	1821	2343	3111	3531
178	230	279	331	438	483	487	663	802	766	802
11,207	13,478	15,986	18,251	21,476	25,187	25,297	26,626	30,399	36,286	38,254
1737	2094	2421	2810	3668	4795	4842	5256	6372	7833	8322
3198	3672	4158	4767	5759	6626	6647	6908	7947	9737	10,255
1978	2192	2516	2701	2930	3226	3239	3428	3934	4673	4893
3078	3826	4822	5639	6485	7606	7631	7897	8712	10,084	10,638
1315	1693	2069	2334	2632	2934	2939	3138	3435	3959	4146
6157	8932	10,347	11,638	12,544	13,260	13,297	13,517	14,061	15,419	15,858
781	1310	1751	2076	2387	2572	2564	2792	2982	3422	3558
1625	1912	2232	2225	2404	2460	2471	2538	2621	2757	2761
2168	2679	3107	3293	3404	3622	3629	3785	3955	4326	4493
37	191	319	577	647	674	681	642	620	634	651
98	349	402	584	637	690	693	643	653	683	688
452	1063	1066	1192	1296	1378	1316	1326	1326	1417	1458
996	1428	1470	1691	1769	1867	1881	1801	1905	2180	2248
13,667	16,093	19,034	22,006	24,325	27,152	27,281	29,805	33,792	38,907	42,247
1513	1656	1854	2062	2309	2425	2422	2678	3319	3987	4428
618	763	959	1221	1464	1717	1729	1902	2006	1856	1817
1649	1859	2147	2290	2417	2606	2615	2486	2945	3045	3175
1542	1768	2021	2185	2338	2604	2617	2916	3292	3577	3939
1400	1618	1894	2206	2559	3133	3170	3572	4062	4567	4935
996	1151	1340	1515	1684	1739	1739	1900	2117	2395	2555
1542	1837	2216	2609	2896	2903	2909	3124	3445	3958	4395
269	391	529	753	968	1445	1468	1897	2771	4997	5794
1263	1513	1829	2138	2348	2644	2646	2833	3062	3276	3489
1132	1290	1551	1797	1791	1998	2010	2184	2179	2185	2321
940	1119	1382	1656	1799	2086	2102	2364	2684	3263	3554
803	1128	1312	1574	1752	1852	1854	1949	1910	1792	1945

Table A-1 (continued)

States and Regions	1790	1800	1810	1820	1830	1840	1850	1860	1870
Southwest	—	—	—	—	—	—	275	698	921
Oklahoma	—	—	—	—	—	—	—	—	—
Texas	—	—	—	—	—	—	213	604	819
New Mexico	—	—	—	—	—	—	62	94	92
Arizona	—	—	—	—	—	—	—	—	10
Rocky Mountain	—	—	—	—	—	—	11	74	172
Montana	—	—	—	—	—	—	—	—	21
Idaho	—	—	—	—	—	—	—	—	15
Wyoming	—	—	—	—	—	—	—	—	9
Colorado	—	—	—	—	—	—	—	34	40
Utah	—	—	—	—	—	—	11	40	87
Far West	—	—	—	—	—	—	106	451	717
Washington	—	—	—	—	—	—	1	12	24
Oregon	—	—	—	—	—	—	12	52	91
Nevada	—	—	—	—	—	—	—	7	42
California	—	—	—	—	—	—	93	380	560
Total, Continental U.S.	3930	5310	7240	9638	12,862	17,063	23,193	31,443	38,561
Alaska									
Hawaii									
Total, U.S.									

Sources: Population for 1790-1950: *Historical Statistics of the United States, Colonial Times to 1957.* Series A-123-180, pp. 12-12. Washington, D.C., 1960.
Population for 1929: Department of Commerce, Office of Business Economics, *Personal Income by States, Since 1929.*
Population for 1960, 1965: Department of Commerce, Bureau of the Census, *Current Population Reports*, Series P-25, nos. 304, 380, and unpublished data.
Indicates total as appears in the cited sources. Other totals computed from state data.

1880	1890	1900	1910	1920	1929	1930	1940	1950	1960	1965
1752	2743	4157	6085	7385	8984	9080	9782	11,375	14,242	15,591
—	259	790	1657	2028	2372	2396	2336	2233	2337	2456
1592	2236	3049	3897	4663	5762	5825	6415	7711	9631	10,547
120	160	195	327	360	420	423	532	681	953	1013
40	88	123	204	334	430	436	499	750	1321	1575
431	919	1315	2020	2564	2710	2753	3008	3485	4349	4664
39	143	243	376	549	524	538	559	591	679	702
33	89	162	326	432	447	445	525	589	671	694
21	63	93	146	194	223	226	251	291	331	331
194	413	540	799	940	1008	1036	1123	1325	1768	1947
144	211	277	373	449	508	508	550	689	900	990
1177	1935	2459	4275	5644	8123	8285	8943	14,646	20,781	23,746
75	357	518	1142	1357	1555	1563	1736	2379	2856	2976
175	318	414	673	783	947	954	1090	1521	1772	1937
62	47	42	82	77	90	91	110	160	291	433
865	1213	1485	2378	3427	5531	5677	6907	10,586	15,862	18,400
50,159	62,947	75,997	91,972	105,711	121,769	122,776	131,308	150,698	179,124	192,836
									228	267
									641	710
									179,993	193,810

Table A-2. *United States per capita personal income by states and regions, 1880-1965* (in current Dollars)

States and Regions	1880	1900	1919-21 Average	1929	1930	1940	1950	1955	1960	1965
New England	246	271	819	876	806	757	1,601	2,030	2,425	3,027
Maine	149	187	611	601	575	523	1,185	1,551	1,844	2,309
New Hampshire	198	214	657	690	648	579	1,323	1,765	2,143	2,581
Vermont	168	190	580	627	569	507	1,121	1,464	1,841	2,377
Massachusetts	292	304	907	913	844	784	1,633	2,026	2,459	3,072
Rhode Island	279	293	849	871	787	743	1,606	1,961	2,211	2,891
Connecticut	268	278	789	1,029	926	917	1,875	2,414	2,807	3,455
Mideast	242	277	858	973	890	790	1,756	2,153	2,565	3,124
New York	280	323	1,020	1,159	1,043	870	1,873	2,283	2,746	3,296
New Jersey	253	277	812	931	859	822	1,834	2,306	2,708	3,260
Pennsylvania	222	250	744	775	716	648	1,541	1,889	2,242	2,755
Delaware	199	220	708	1,017	849	1,004	2,131	2,519	2,757	3,346
Maryland	171	204	726	777	719	712	1,602	1,994	2,343	3,027
District of Columbia				1,273	1,262	1,170	2,221	2,483	3,017	3,694
Great Lakes	178	216	717	803	684	667	1,660	2,095	2,383	3,011
Michigan	175	185	719	793	659	679	1,700	2,183	2,324	3,052
Ohio	177	222	707	781	671	665	1,620	2,081	2,334	2,859
Indiana	150	182	582	612	519	553	1,512	1,894	2,188	2,860
Illinois	208	260	829	957	816	754	1,825	2,243	2,650	3,304
Wisconsin	156	179	608	682	595	554	1,477	1,816	2,175	2,733

Table A-2 (continued)

States and Regions	1880	1900	1919-21 Average	1929	1930	1940	1950	1955	1960	1965
Plains	157	197	567	572	510	483	1,428	1,681	2,067	2,647
Minnesota	175	207	574	598	552	526	1,410	1,729	2,116	2,683
Iowa	168	202	564	577	507	501	1,485	1,608	1,986	2,741
Missouri	157	188	584	628	569	524	1,431	1,802	2,115	2,662
North Dakota	186	209	458	375	305	350	1,263	1,379	1,715	2,311
South Dakota		183	539	417	358	359	1,243	1,293	1,782	2,220
Nebraska	156	212	557	590	517	439	1,491	1,593	2,110	2,643
Kansas	120	187	588	535	468	426	1,443	1,732	2,161	2,678
Southeast	87	97	371	368	313	343	1,022	1,343	1,610	2,103
Virginia	85	110	420	435	384	466	1,228	1,571	1,841	2,422
West Virginia	89	117	513	462	411	407	1,065	1,326	1,594	2,029
Kentucky	107	120	420	391	325	320	981	1,329	1,574	2,058
Tennessee	81	101	361	377	325	339	994	1,281	1,543	2,047
North Carolina	64	72	354	334	293	328	1,037	1,313	1,561	2,054
South Carolina	72	74	336	270	241	307	893	1,181	1,377	1,852
Georgia	86	86	348	350	308	340	1,034	1,375	1,639	2,171
Florida	79	112	437	521	464	513	1,281	1,630	1,950	2,450
Alabama	82	88	313	324	266	282	880	1,233	1,488	1,923
Mississippi	82	84	281	285	203	218	755	1,020	1,205	1,615
Louisiana	138	128	426	415	358	363	1,120	1,396	1,655	2,084
Arkansas	79	89	329	305	223	256	825	1,142	1,372	1,839
Southwest	106	139	534	474	401	418	1,297	1,629	1,922	2,348
Oklahoma	m	114	504	454	368	373	1,143	1,507	1,861	2,303
Texas	98	138	539	478	411	432	1,349	1,667	1,925	2,360
New Mexico	105	148	477	407	333	375	1,177	1,504	1,890	2,240
Arizona	399	321	701	591	514	497	1,331	1,677	2,032	2,400

Table A-2 (continued)

States and Regions	1880	1900	1919-21 Average	1929	1930	1940	1950	1955	1960	1965
Rocky Mountain	290	296	667	596	538	531	1,457	1,742	2,108	2,552
Montana	456	415	627	595	503	570	1,622	1,852	2,037	2,455
Idaho	281	221	597	503	497	464	1,295	1,539	1,849	2,409
Wyoming	321	311	902	677	584	608	1,669	1,857	2,263	2,570
Colorado	371	318	728	637	580	546	1,487	1,814	2,275	2,723
Utah	134	183	556	559	505	487	1,309	1,625	1,968	2,379
Far West	370	332	907	910	816	785	1,801	2,239	2,622	3,188
Washington	234	296	770	750	665	662	1,674	2,038	2,349	2,913
Oregon	234	248	744	683	620	623	1,620	1,928	2,235	2,771
Nevada	606	395	939	878	826	876	2,019	2,549	2,856	3,329
California	392	365	998	995	889	840	1,852	2,313	2,710	3,274
Total, Continental U.S.	186	195	498	703	624	595	1,496	1,876	2,213	2,764
Alaska									2,846	3,214
Hawaii									2,369	2,863
Total, U.S.									2,215	2,765

Table A-2 United States per capita personal income by States and Regions, 1880-1965. (In Current Dollars)

Sources: Personal income per capita for 1880-1920: Everett S. Lee, Ann Ratner Miller and Carol P. Brainard, Richard A. Easterlin, *Population Redistribution and Economic Growth, United States, 1870-1950*. Vol. I, The American Philosophical Society, Independence Square. Philadelphia (Pa.), 1960.

Personal income per capita for 1929-40: Department of Commerce, Office of Business Economics, *Survey of Current Business*. August 1968, vol. 48, no. 8.

The regional personal income per capita figures for 1880-1920 were obtained by summing the personal income totals for each state in the region (as given in *Population Redistribution...*) and dividing by the regional population (as given in *Population Redistribution...*).

Table A-3 *United States per capita personal income, by states and regions, 1880-1965* (1957-59 = 100)

(In Constant Dollars)

States and Regions	1880	1920	1930	1940	1950	1960	1965
New England	942	1173	1385	1551	1911	2352	2754
Maine	571	875	988	1072	1414	1789	2101
New Hampshire	758	941	1113	1186	1579	2079	2348
Vermont	643	831	978	1039	1338	1786	2163
Massachusetts	1118	1299	1450	1607	1949	2385	2795
Rhode Island	1069	1216	1352	1523	1916	2145	2565
Connecticut	1026	1130	1591	1879	2237	2723	3144
Mideast	927	1229	1529	1619	2095	2488	2843
New York	1072	1470	1792	1783	2235	2663	2999
New Jersey	969	1163	1476	1684	2189	2627	2966
Pennsylvania	850	1066	1230	1328	1839	2175	2507
Delaware	762	1014	1459	2057	2543	2674	3045
Maryland	655	1040	1235	1459	1912	2273	2754
District of Columbia			2168	2398	2650	2926	3361
Great Lakes	682	1027	1175	1367	1988	2311	2740
Michigan	670	1030	1132	1391	2029	2254	2777
Ohio	678	1013	1153	1363	1933	2264	2601
Indiana	575	834	892	1133	1804	2122	2602
Illinois	797	1188	1402	1545	2178	2570	3006
Wisconsin	597	871	1022	1135	1763	2110	2487
Plains	601	812	876	990	1704	2005	2409
Minnesota	760	822	948	1078	1683	2052	2441
Iowa	643	808	871	1027	1772	1926	2494
Missouri	601	837	978	1074	1708	2051	2422
North Dakota	712	656	524	717	1507	1663	2103
South Dakota		772	615	736	1483	1728	2020
Nebraska	597	798	888	900	1779	2047	2405
Kansas	460	842	804	873	1722	2096	2437
Southeast	333	532	538	703	1220	1562	1914
Virginia	326	602	660	955	1465	1786	2204
West Virginia	341	735	706	834	1271	1546	1846
Kentucky	410	573	558	656	1171	1527	1873
Tennessee	310	517	558	695	1186	1497	1863
North Carolina	245	507	503	672	1237	1514	1869
South Carolina	276	481	414	629	1066	1336	1685
Georgia	329	499	529	697	1234	1590	1975
Florida	303	626	797	1051	1529	1891	2229
Alabama	314	448	457	578	1050	1443	1750
Mississippi	314	403	349	447	901	1169	1470
Louisiana	529	610	615	744	1337	1605	1896
Arkansas	303	471	383	525	984	1331	1673

Table A-3 (continued)

States and Regions	1880	1920	1930	1940	1950	1960	1965
Southwest	406	765	689	857	1548	1864	2136
Oklahoma		722	632	764	1364	1805	2096
Texas	375	772	706	885	1610	1867	2147
New Mexico	402	683	572	768	1405	1833	2038
Arizona	1528	1004	883	1018	1588	1971	2184
Rocky Mountain	1111	956	924	1088	1739	2045	2322
Montana	1746	898	864	1168	1936	1976	2234
Idaho	1076	855	854	951	1545	1793	2192
Wyoming	1229	1292	1003	1246	1992	2195	2338
Colorado	1421	1043	997	1119	1774	2207	2478
Utah	513	797	868	998	1562	1909	2165
Far West	1417	1299	1402	1609	2149	2543	2901
Washington	896	1103	1143	1357	1998	2278	2651
Oregon	896	1066	1065	1277	1933	2168	2521
Nevada	2321	1345	1419	1795	2409	2770	3029
California	1501	1430	1527	1721	2210	2629	2979
Total, Continental U.S.	676	713	1072	1219	1785	2146	2515
Alaska						2760	2924
Hawaii						2298	2605
Total, United States						2148	2516

Sources: Table A-2 for base personal income data.

Price indices: A consumer price index available from the 1968 U.S. Statistical Abstract (Table 505, p. 347) for years 1915-1967 in 1957-69 prices was used to convert 1920-1965 current dollars to 1957-69 constant dollars. Data for 1880 were price-adjusted as follows: the price movement from 1880-1913 was estimated by averaging the Federal Bank of New York and Burgess Cost of Living indices (both have 1913 base). These are taken from *United States Historical Statistics, Colonial Times to 1957*. Series E157-60, p. 127. Price movements for 1913-1920 were estimated from United States Historical Statistics' table, Series E113-139. Price movements for 1920 to 1957-59 were estimated through use of the Statistical Abstract Table 505, p. 347, as above.

The divisors used to convert current to constant dollars are listed below:

1880	.261
1920	.698
1930	.582
1940	.488
1950	.838
1960	1.031
1965	1.099

Table A-4. *Per cent of total United States population by region and state*

States and Regions	1790	1800	1810	1820	1830	1840	1850
New England	25.7	23.2	20.3	17.2	15.2	13.1	11.8
Maine	2.5	2.9	3.2	3.1	3.1	2.9	2.5
New Hampshire	3.6	3.5	3.0	2.5	2.1	1.7	1.4
Vermont	2.2	2.9	3.0	2.4	2.2	1.7	1.4
Massachusetts	9.6	8.0	6.5	5.4	4.7	4.3	4.3
Rhode Island	1.8	1.3	1.1	.9	.8	.6	.6
Connecticut	6.1	4.7	3.6	2.9	2.3	1.8	1.6
Mideast	34.0	34.2	34.3	33.2	32.2	29.9	28.6
New York	8.7	11.1	13.2	14.2	14.9	14.2	13.4
New Jersey	4.7	4.0	3.4	2.9	2.5	2.2	2.1
Pennsylvania	11.0	11.3	11.2	10.9	10.5	10.1	10.0
Delaware	1.5	1.2	1.0	.8	.6	.5	.4
Maryland	8.1	6.4	5.3	4.2	3.5	2.8	2.5
District of Columbia	—	.2	.2	.2	.2	.2	.2
Great Lakes	—	1.0	3.8	8.2	11.4	17.1	19.5
Michigan	—	—	.1	.1	.2	1.2	1.7
Ohio	—	.8	3.2	6.0	7.3	8.9	8.5
Indiana	—	.1	.3	1.5	2.7	4.0	4.3
Illinois	—	—	.2	.6	1.2	2.8	3.7
Wisconsin	—	—	—	—	—	.2	1.3
Plains	—	—	.3	.7	1.1	2.5	3.8
Minnesota	—	—	—	—	—	—	—
Iowa	—	—	—	—	—	.3	.8
Missouri	—	—	.3	.7	1.1	2.3	2.9
North Dakota	—	—	—	—	—	—	—
South Dakota	—	—	—	—	—	—	—
Nebraska	—	—	—	—	—	—	—
Kansas	—	—	—	—	—	—	—
Southeast	40.3	41.6	41.3	40.6	40.1	37.3	34.7
Virginia	17.6	15.2	12.2	9.7	8.1	6.0	4.8
West Virginia	1.4	1.5	1.5	1.4	1.4	1.3	1.3
Kentucky	1.9	4.2	5.6	5.9	5.3	4.6	4.2
Tennessee	.9	2.0	3.6	4.4	5.3	4.9	4.3
North Carolina	10.0	9.0	7.7	6.6	5.7	4.4	3.7
South Carolina	6.3	6.5	5.7	5.2	4.5	3.5	2.9
Georgia	2.1	3.1	3.5	3.5	4.0	4.0	3.9
Florida	—	—	—	—	.3	.3	.4
Alabama	—	—	.1	1.3	2.4	3.5	3.3
Mississippi	—	.2	.4	.8	1.1	2.2	2.6
Louisiana	—	—	1.1	1.6	1.7	2.1	2.2
Arkansas	—	—	—	.1	.2	.6	.9

1860	1870	1880	1890	1900	1910	1920	1930	1940	1950	1960
10.0	9.0	8.0	7.5	7.4	7.1	7.0	6.7	6.4	6.2	5.8
2.0	1.6	1.3	1.1	.9	.8	.7	.6	.6	.6	.5
1.0	.8	.7	.6	.5	.5	.4	.4	.4	.4	.3
1.0	.9	.7	.5	.5	.4	.3	.3	.3	.3	.2
3.9	3.8	3.6	3.6	3.7	3.7	3.6	3.5	3.3	3.1	2.9
.6	.6	.6	.5	.6	.6	.6	.6	.5	.5	.5
1.5	1.4	1.2	1.2	1.2	1.2	1.3	1.3	1.3	1.3	1.4
26.5	25.5	23.4	22.5	22.5	23.0	23.1	23.3	23.1	22.3	21.5
12.3	11.4	10.1	9.5	9.6	9.9	9.8	10.3	10.3	9.8	9.4
2.1	2.3	2.3	2.3	2.5	2.8	3.0	3.3	3.2	3.2	3.4
9.2	9.1	8.5	8.4	8.3	8.3	8.2	7.8	7.5	7.0	6.3
.4	.3	.3	.3	.2	.2	.2	.2	.2	.2	.2
2.2	2.0	1.9	1.7	1.6	1.4	1.4	1.3	1.4	1.6	1.7
.2	.3	.4	.4	.4	.4	.4	.4	.5	.5	
22.0	23.6	22.3	21.4	21.0	19.8	20.3	20.6	20.3	20.2	20.2
2.4	3.1	3.3	3.3	3.2	3.1	3.5	3.9	4.0	4.2	4.4
7.4	6.9	6.4	5.8	5.5	5.1	5.4	5.4	5.3	5.3	5.4
4.3	4.4	3.9	3.5	3.3	2.9	2.8	2.6	2.6	2.6	2.6
5.4	6.6	6.1	6.1	6.3	6.1	6.1	6.2	6.0	5.8	5.6
2.5	2.7	2.6	2.7	2.7	2.5	2.5	2.4	2.4	2.3	2.2
6.9	10.0	12.3	14.2	13.6	12.7	11.9	10.8	10.3	9.3	8.6
.5	1.1	1.6	2.1	2.3	2.3	2.3	2.1	2.1	2.0	1.9
2.1	3.1	3.2	3.0	2.9	2.4	2.3	2.0	1.9	1.7	1.5
3.8	4.5	4.3	4.3	4.1	3.6	3.2	3.0	2.9	2.6	2.4
—	—	.1	.3	.4	.6	.6	.6	.5	.4	.4
—	—	.2	.6	.5	.6	.6	.6	.5	.4	.4
.1	.3	.9	1.7	1.4	1.3	1.2	1.1	1.0	.9	.8
.3	.9	2.0	2.3	1.9	1.8	1.7	1.5	1.4	1.3	1.2
30.7	27.0	27.2	25.6	25.0	23.9	23.0	22.2	22.7	22.4	21.6
3.9	3.2	3.0	2.6	2.4	2.2	2.2	2.0	2.0	2.2	2.2
1.2	1.1	1.2	1.2	1.3	1.3	1.4	1.4	1.4	1.2	1.0
3.7	3.4	3.3	3.0	2.8	2.5	2.3	2.1	1.9	2.0	1.7
3.5	3.3	3.1	2.8	2.7	2.4	2.2	2.1	2.2	2.2	2.0
3.2	2.8	2.8	2.6	2.5	2.4	2.4	2.6	2.7	2.7	2.5
2.2	1.8	2.0	1.8	1.8	1.6	1.6	1.4	1.4	1.4	1.3
3.4	3.1	3.1	2.9	2.9	2.8	2.7	2.4	2.4	2.3	2.2
.4	.5	.5	.6	.7	.8	.9	1.2	1.4	1.8	2.8
3.1	2.6	2.5	2.4	2.4	2.3	2.2	2.2	2.2	2.0	1.8
2.5	2.1	2.3	2.0	2.0	2.0	1.7	1.6	1.7	1.4	1.2
2.3	1.9	1.9	1.8	1.8	1.8	1.7	1.7	1.8	1.8	1.8
1.4	1.3	1.6	1.8	1.7	1.7	1.7	1.5	1.5	1.3	1.0

Table A-4 (continued)

States and Regions	1790	1800	1810	1820	1830	1840	1850
Southwest	—	—	—	—	—	—	1.2
Oklahoma	—	—	—	—	—	—	—
Texas	—	—	—	—	—	—	.9
New Mexico	—	—	—	—	—	—	.3
Arizona	—	—	—	—	—	—	—
Rocky Mountain	—	—	—	—	—	—	—
Montana	—	—	—	—	—	—	—
Idaho	—	—	—	—	—	—	—
Wyoming	—	—	—	—	—	—	—
Colorado	—	—	—	—	—	—	—
Utah	—	—	—	—	—	—	—
Far West	—	—	—	—	—	—	.5
Washington	—	—	—	—	—	—	—
Oregon	—	—	—	—	—	—	.1
Nevada	—	—	—	—	—	—	—
California	—	—	—	—	—	—	.4
Total, Continental U.S.	100.0	100.0	100.0	99.9	100.0	99.9	100.1
Alaska	—	—	—	—	—	—	—
Hawaii	—	—	—	—	—	—	—
Total, U.S.	100.0	100.0	100.0	99.9	100.0	99.9	100.1

Sources: 1790-1950: United States Bureau of the Census, *Historical Statistics of the United States, Colonial Times to 1957*. Washington, D.C. 1960.
1950,* 1960:* Department of Commerce, Bureau of the Census: *United States Census of Population*. 1950, Vol. II and 1960, Vol. I.

Note: Indicates use of 1950 urban definition. All other figures derived from the 1940 definition.

1860	1870	1880	1890	1900	1910	1920	1930	1940	1950	1960
2.2	2.4	3.5	4.4	5.5	6.6	7.0	7.4	7.4	7.5	7.9
—	—	—	.4	1.0	1.8	1.9	2.0	1.8	1.5	1.3
1.9	2.1	3.2	3.6	4.0	4.2	4.4	4.7	4.9	5.1	5.4
.3	.2	.2	.3	.4	.3	.3	.4	.5	.5	.5
—	—	.1	.1	.2	.2	.3	.4	.4	.5	.7
.2	.4	.9	1.5	1.7	2.2	2.4	2.2	2.3	2.3	2.4
—	.1	.1	.2	.3	.4	.5	.4	.4	.4	.4
—	—	.1	.1	.2	.4	.4	.4	.4	.4	.4
—	—	—	.1	.1	.2	.2	.2	.2	.2	.2
.1	.1	.4	.7	.7	.9	.8	.9	.9	.9	1.0
.1	.2	.3	.3	.4	.4	.4	.4	.4	.5	.5
1.4	1.9	2.3	3.1	3.2	4.6	5.3	6.7	7.5	9.7	11.5
—	.1	.1	.6	.7	1.2	1.3	1.3	1.3	1.6	1.6
.2	.2	.3	.5	.5	.7	.7	.8	.8	1.0	1.0
—	.1	.1	.1	.1	.1	.1	.1	.1	.1	.2
1.2	1.5	1.7	1.9	2.0	2.6	3.2	4.6	5.3	7.0	8.8
99.9	99.8	99.9	100.2	99.9	99.9	100.0	99.9	100.0	99.9	99.5
—	—	—	—	—	—	—	—	—	—	.1
—	—	—	—	—	—	—	—	—	—	.4
99.9	99.8	99.9	100.2	99.9	99.9	100.0	99.9	100.0	99.9	100.0

Table A-5. *Population by residence, urban and rural*

Year	Urban	Rural		Urban	Rural	
		Non-farm	Farm		Non-farm	Farm
	(in thousands)			(per cent)		
1790	202	3,728		5.1	94.9	
1800	322	4,986		6.1	93.9	
1810	525	6,714		7.3	92.7	
1820	693	8,945		7.2	92.8	
1830	1,127	11,739		8.8	91.2	
1840	1,845	15,224		10.8	89.2	
1850	3,544	19,648		15.3	84.7	
1860	6,217	25,227		19.8	80.2	
1870	9,902	28,656		25.7	74.3	
1880	14,130	36,026		28.2	71.8	
1890	22,106	40,841		35.1	64.9	
1900	30,160	45,835		39.7	60.3	
1910	41,999	49,973		45.7	54.3	
1920	54,158	20.159	31,393	51.2	19.1	29.7
1930	68,955	23,663	30,158	56.2	19.3	24.6
1940	74,424	27,029	30,216	56.5	20.5	22.9
1950	88,927	38,693	23,077	59.0	25.7	15.3
1950*	96,847	31,431	23,048	64.0	20.8	15.2
1960*	125,284	40,567	13,474	69.9	22.6	7.5

* Indicates use of 1950 urban definition. All other figures derived from the 1940 definition.

Sources: Table A-4, p. 160.

APPENDIX B

Research needs

Throughout the preparation of the series of international studies of regional development, of which this is one, Dr. Antoni R. Kuklinski, Programme Director of Regional Development of the United Nations Research Institute for Social Development, has emphasized the importance of identifying the research needs which must be filled in order to support improvement in future performance.

One conclusion which appears inescapable is that improvement of future regional development efforts to meet human objectives will require large increases in research efforts to permit the public and the government to choose wisely between the claims and counterclaims of the developers and conservationists, the technologists and the environmentalists, and between the proponents of growth and the advocates of qualitative change. Because of the fundamental relationships of these issues to the quality of human life, heavy investment in basic and applied research is probably the single most important need in upgrading regional and urban development.

With these needs in mind, the author of this study has worked closely with Professor T. N. Brewis of Carlton University, Ottawa, who has prepared the comparison study of Canadian regional development which will round out the survey of the North American approach to this problem. The two studies have not pointed towards an exact identity in future research needs, but the similarity has been sufficiently close to suggest a joint effort in presenting our views on future research needs. The list that follows is not exhaustive, but represents an effort to identify some major priorities in research on North American regional development.

Some research priorities

Improving the performance of regional and national economies in achieving goals of social justice and equity.

Design of guidelines and policies to channel interregional development competition into directions which serve regional and national policy objectives.

International cooperation to establish global policies for economic development and environmental management.

The evaluation of goals in regional development and analysis of benefits and costs of alternative methods for achieving development goals.

The design and role of incentives in encouraging optimal interregional distribution of population, migration, and economic activity.

Improving housing, transportation, personal safety, and the general quality of life in urban regions.

The pollution and environmental characteristics of specific production and consumption activities as a function of activity levels, alternative pollution abatement methods and the evaluation of benefits and costs of alternative pollution abatement techniques.

The role of growth centers in regional development and criteria for their selection.

The design of industrial complexes and analysis of the determinants of successful operation.

The design of environmentally neutral residential, commercial, and industrial complexes, planned for maximum recycling of wastes and economic consumption of residuals.

The concept of optimal size and distribution of population as related to human objectives, ecological balance, and environmental management. Implications of alternative population distribution between urban, suburban, and rural locations. Determinants of economies of scale and quality of service in public sector programs.

Planning and assessment of technological systems in advance of introduction in order to minimize damaging indirect effects and to harness technology to the service of social priorities.

The design of life cycle planning in resource development in order to achieve environmental safety during the exploration, exploitation, and restoration of natural resource deposits.

The coordinated use of market factors, financial incentives, tax structures, planning and zoning procedures to encourage optimal land use.

The development of consistent coordinated national policies in the related areas of regional development, urban redevelopment, migration planning, housing, transportation, technology assessment, land use, resource management, and environmental design.

Bibliography and references

Aaron, Henry J., 1969. 'Income transfer problems.' *Monthly Labor Review*, 92, pp. 50-54.

Andeano, Ralph (ed.), 1962. *The Economic Impact of the American Civil War*. Cambridge, Schenkman.

Appalachian Regional Commission (ARC), 1968. *Annual Report, 1968*. Washington, D.C. See also: Jones and Widner, 1969; Newman, 1969; Widner *et al.* 1969.

Battelle Memorial Institute, 1964. *A Dynamic Model of the Economy of the Susquehanna River Basin*. Columbus (Ohio), Batelle Memorial Institute.

Behan, R. W., 1967. 'The Succotash syndrome, or multiple use: A heartfelt approach to forest land management.' *Natural Resources Journal*, vol. 4, pp. 473-484.

Bergmann, Barbara R.; Chinitz, Benjamin; and Hoover, Edgar M., 1961. *Projection of a Metropolis: Technical Supplement to the New York Metropolitan Region Study*. Cambridge, Harvard University Press.

Berry, Brian L. J., 1969. *Growth Centers and their Potentials in the Upper Great Lakes Region*. Washington, D.C. Upper Great Lakes Regional Commission.

Boulding, Kenneth E., 1950. *A Reconstruction of Economics*. New York, John Wiley.

—, 1967. *The Role of Legitimacy in the Dynamics of Society*. Pennsylvania State University, University Center for Research of the College of Business Administration.

Brewer, W. D., 1969. *Early Action Economic Development Program*. Washington, D.C. Four Corner Regional Commission.

Brewis, T. N., 1969. *Regional Economic Policies in Canada*. Toronto, Macmillan.

Brewster, John M., 1963. 'The relevance of the Jeffersonian dream today.' in Ottoson, Howard W. (ed.), *Land Use Policy and Problems in the United States*. Lincoln, University of Nebraska Press.

Cameron, G. C., 1969a. 'The regional problem in the United States: Some reflections on a viable federal strategy.' *Regional Studies*, vol. 2, pp. 207-220.

—, 1969b. 'Regional development: The federal role.' Monograph submitted to Resources for the Future Inc.

Carter, Luther J., 1966. 'North Slope: Oil Rush.' *Science*, vol. 166, pp. 85-92.

Caudill, Harry M., 1963. *Night Comes to the Cumberlands*. Boston, Little, Brown and Co.

Chandler, John H., 1969. 'An international comparison.' *Monthly Labour Review*, pp. 55-56.

Chinard, Gilbert, 1939. *Thomas Jefferson*. Boston, Little, Brown and Co.

Chinitz, Benjamin, 1960. *Freight and the Metropolis*. Cambridge, Harvard University Press.

Clapp, Gordon R., 1955. *The TVA. An Approach to the Development of a Region.* Chicago, University of Chicago Press.

Clawson, Marion, 1963a. 'Public and private interest for public lands.' In Ottoson, Howard W. (ed.), *Land Use Policy and Problems in the United States.* Lincoln, University of Nebraska Press.

—, 1963b. *Land and Water for Recreation: Opportunities, Problems and Policies.* Chicago, Rand McNally.

—, 1967. *The Federal Lands since 1956: Recent Trends in Use and Management.* Washington, D.C., Resources for the Future Inc.

Cleary, Edward J., 1967. *The Orsanco Story.* Baltimore, Johns Hopkins Press.

Coastal Plains Regional Commission (CPRC), 1968. *Regional Development Plan.* Washington, D.C., Coastal Plains Regional Commission.

Committee for Economic Development, 1964. *Community Economic Development Efforts: Five Case Studies.* New York, Committee for Economic Development.

Coulter, James B., 1968. *Marine Shipping Industry: Effects and Impacts on the Chesapeake Bay.* Proceedings of the Governor's Conference on the Chesapeake Bay, Annapolis (Maryland), September 12-13, 1968.

Cumberland, John H., 1966. 'A regional interindustry model for the analysis of development objectives.' *Regional Sciences Association Papers*, vol. 17, pp. 65-94.

—, and Van Beek, Fritz, 1967. 'Regional development objectives and subsidization of local industry.' *Land Economics*, vol. 43, pp. 253-264.

—, and Hibbs, James R., 1970. *Alternative Future Environments.* Paper presented before the Institute of Managements Sciences at the National Bureau of Standards. Gaithersburg (Maryland), March 1970.

Curtis, Richard and Hogan, Elizabeth, 1969. *Perils of Peaceful Atom.* New York, Doubleday.

Dasmann, Raymond F., 1965. *The Destruction of California.* New York, Macmillan.

Davis, Lance E.; Hughes, Jonathan R. T.; and McDougall, Duncan M., 1961. *American Economic History: The Development of a National Economy.* Homewood (Ill.), Irwin.

De Tocqueville, Alexis, 1838. *Democracy in America.* Translated by Henry Reeve. New York, George Adlard.

—, 1959. *Journey to America* (First published 1833). Edited by J. P. Meyer; translated by George Lawrence. London, Faber and Faber.

Dillard, Dudley, 1967. *Economic Development of the North Atlantic Community.* Englewood Cliffs (N.J.), Prentice-Hall.

Dillon, Conley H., 1964. *The Area Redevelopment Administration: New Patterns in Developmental Administration.* College Park (Maryland), University of Maryland, Bureau of Governmental Research.

Dodge, Norton T. and Cumberland, John H., 1970. *Some Environmental Externalities in Regional Development: A Refinery Case Study.* University of Maryland, Bureau of Business and Economic Research. Also in: *Review of Regional Studies*, vol. 1, no. 1 (November, 1970), pp. 49-59.

Droze, W. H., 1965. *High Dams and Slack Water, The TVA Rebuilds a River.* Baton Rouge (La.).

Ellis, David M., 1964. 'The railroads and their land grants.' In Nash, Gerald D. (ed.), *Issues in American Economic History.* Boston, Heath.

Fagin, Henry, 19.... 'The Penn-Jersey Transportation study: The launching of a permanent regional planning process.' *Journal of the American Institute of Planners*, 29, pp. 10-18.

Finer, Herman, 1964. *The TVA: Lessons for International Application.* Montreal, International Labour Office.

Fishlow, Albert, 1965. 'American railroads and the transformation of the Ante-Bellum economy.' *Harvard Economic Studies*, vol. 127.

Flora, A.C., 1968. 'A new regional concept of economic development.' *Business and Economic Review*, vol. XIV, no. 9 (June). Columbia, University of South Carolina. Bureau of Business and Economic Research.

Fogelson, Robert M., 1967. *The Fragmented Metropolis: Los Angeles, 1890-1930*. Cambridge, Harvard University Press.

Four Corners Regional Commission (FCRC). 1969. *First Annual Report, 1968*. See also: Brewer, 1969.

Friedman, John, 1966. 'Poor regions and poor nations: Perspectives on the problem of Appalachia.' *Southern Economic Journal*, 32, no. 4, pp. 465-473.

Gallatin, Albert, 1968. *Report of the Secretary of the Treasury on the Subject of Public Roads and Canals* (First published, Washington, 1808). Reprinted edition, New York, Augustus M. Kelly.

Gardner, Richard N. and Millikan, Max F. (eds.), 1968. *The Global Partnership: International Agencies and Economic Development*. New York, Praeger.

Gaskins, Darius; Liner, Donald C.; and Miller, Stanley, 1968. 'Evaluation of business loan programs of the economic development administration and the area redevelopment administration.' *Research Review*, October, pp. 1-14.

Gates, Paul W., 1963. 'The Homestead Act: Free land policy in operation, 1862-1935.' In Ottoson, Howard W. (ed.), *Land Use Policy and Problems in the United States*. Lincoln, University of Nebraska Press.

—, 1968. *History of Public Law Development*. Written for the Public Land Law Review Commission, with a chapter by Robert W. Swenson, Washington, D.C., U.S. Government Printing Office.

Goodrich, Carter, 1960. *Government Promotion of American Canals and Railroads, 1800-1890*. New York, Columbia University Press.

— *et al.*, 1961. *Canals and American Economic Development*. New York, Columbia University Press.

— (ed.), 1967. *The Government and the Economy, 1783-1861*. New York, Bobbs-Merrill.

Griswold, Whitney, 1964. 'Three puritans on prosperity.' In Nash, Gerald D. (ed.), *Issues in American History*. Boston, Heath.

Hagen, Everett E., 1962. *On the Theory of Social Change: How Economic Growth Begins*. Homewood (Ill.), The Dorsey Press.

Hale, Carl W., 1969. 'The optimality of local subsidies in regional development programs.' *The Quarterly Review of Economics and Business*, vol. 9, pp. 35-50.

Hansen, Niles M., 1968. *French Regional Planning*. Bloomington (Ind.), Indiana University Press.

Hendersen, James M. and Krueger, Anne O., 1965. With Rodd, R. Stephen and Adams, John S. *National Growth and Economic Change in the Upper Midwest*. Minneapolis (Minn.), University of Minnesota Press.

Henry, Robert S., 1964. 'The Railroad Grant Legend.' In Nash, Gerald D. (ed.), *Issues in American Economic History*. Boston, Heath.

Hibbard, B. H., 1939. *A History of Public Land Policies*. Magnolia (Mass.), Peter Smith.

Hill, Forest G., 1957. *Roads, Rails and Waterways*. Norman (Okl.), University of Oklahoma Press.

Hoover, Edgar M., 1948. *The Location of Economic Activity*. New York, McGraw-Hill.

— and Vernon R., 1959. *Anatomy of a Metropolis*. Cambridge, Harvard University Press.

—, 1969. 'Some old and new issues in regional development.' in Robinson, E. A. G. (ed.), *Backward Areas in Advanced Countries*. London, Macmillan.

Isard, Walter, 1959. *Methods of Regional Analysis*. Cambridge, John Wiley.
—, 1960. *Location and Space Economy*. Cambridge, John Wiley.
Johnson, E. A. J., 1964. 'Economic ideas of John Winthrop.' In Nash, Gerald D. (ed.), *Issues in American Economic History*, Boston, Heath.
Jones, Clifford L. and Widner, Ralph R., 1969. *Evaluation of the Appalachian Regional Development Program and Its Possible Implications for a New Approach to Federal-State-Local Relationships and Federal Grants-in-Aid*. Washington, D.C. Appalachian Regional Commission.
Kates, Robert W., 1962. *Hazard and Choice Perception in Flood Plain Management*. Research Paper, no. 79. Chicago, University of Chicago Press.
Kelso, M. M., 1963. 'Resolving land use conflicts.' In Ottoson, Howard W. (ed.), *Land Use Policy and Problems in the United States*. Lincoln, University of Nebraska Press.
Kristjenson, Kris and Penn, Raymond J., 1963. 'Public interest in private lands: Private and public conflicts.' In Ottoson, Howard W. (ed.), *Land Use Policy and Problems in the United States*. Lincoln, University of Nebraska Press.
Krutilla, John V., 1967. 'Conservation reconsidered.' *American Economic Review*, vol. 56, no. 4, pp. 777-786.
Kuznets, Simon, and Thomas, Dorothy Swaine, 1960, with Richard A. Easterlin. *Population Redistribution and Economic Growth: United States, 1870-1950*. Philadelphia, American Philosophical Society.
LeDuc, Thomas, 1963. 'History and appraisal of United States land policy until 1862.' In Ottoson, Howard W. (ed.), *Land Use Policy and Problems in the United States*. Lincoln, University of Nebraska Press.
Levitan, Sar. A., 1964. *Federal Aid to Depressed Areas*. Baltimore, Johns Hopkins Press.
Lilienthal, David E., 1944. *TVA: Democracy on the March*. New York, Harper and Brothers.
Lowry, Ira S., 1963. *Portrait of a Region*. Pittsburgh, University of Pittsburgh Press.
Maas, Arthur, 1951. *Muddy Waters; The Army Engineers and the Nation's Rivers*. Cambridge, Harvard University Press.
Macy, Bruce Ward and Hartz, Clyde D. 'Coordination of federal programs in regional planning.' In *Midwest Research Institute Final Report*. No. 2976-D. Kansas City (Mo.), Midwest Research Institute.
McGuire, Martin C. and Garn, Harvey A., forthcoming (a). 'An experiment in the integration of equity and efficiency criteria in public project selection.' *Economic Journal*.
— and Harris, Curtis C., forthcoming (b). 'Migration, economic growth and local unemployment.' *Journal of Human Resources*.
McMillion, Ovid Miller, 1961. *Plant Location Factors and Industrial Land Requirements in the Baltimore Industrial Area*. Unpublished Ph. D. Dissertation. College Park, University of Maryland.
Meyer, John R., 1963. 'Regional economics: A survey.' *American Economic Review*, vol. 53, pp. 17-54.
Mishan, E. J., 1967. *The Costs of Economic Growth*. London, Staples Press.
Moes, John E., 1967. *Local Subsidies for Industry*, Chapel Hill (N. Car.), University of North Carolina Press.
Moore, John R. (ed.), 1967. *The Economic Impact of TVA*. Knoxville (Tenn.), University of Tennessee Press.
Nash, Gerald D. (ed.), 1964. *Issues in American Economic History*. Boston, Heath.
Neale, Walter, 1963. 'Developing countries: Role of land policy in providing incentives for development and sharing more widely the benefits of development.' In Ottoson,

Howard W. (ed.), *Land Use Policy and Problems in the United States*. Lincoln, University of Nebraska Press.

New England Regional Commission (NERC), 1969. *Regional Development Plan*. Draft Report.

New York Times, 1965, 7th January, p. 33.

Newman, D. K., 1969. 'Changing attitudes about the poor.' *Monthly Labor Review*, vol. 92, pp. 32-36.

Newman, M., 1969. *Strategy for Public Policy: The Appalachian Experience*. Paper presented at the Meetings of the Southeastern Regional Science Association. Chapel Hill (N. Car.).

North, Douglass C., 1961. *The Economic Growth of the United States, 1790-1860*. Englewood Cliffs (N.J.), Prentice-Hall.

Northrop, F. S. C., 1946. *The Meeting of East and West*. New York, Collier Books.

Novick, Sheldon, 1969. *The Careless Atom*. Boston, Houghton Mifflin.

Olson, M. *et al.*, 1969. *Towards a Social Report*. U.S. Department of Health, Education and Welfare. Washington, D.C., U.S. Government Printing Office.

Ottoson, Howard W. (ed.), 1963. *Land Use Policy and Problems in the United States*. Lincoln, University of Nebraska Press.

Ozarks Regional Commission (ORC), 1969. *Annual Report 1968*. Washington, D.C., Ozarks Regional Commission.

Perloff, Harvey S. *et al.*, 1966. *Design for a Worldwide Study of Regional Development*. A Report to the United Nations on a Proposed Research Training Program. Baltimore, Johns Hopkins Press.

— *et al.*, 1968a. *Regions, Resources and Economic Growth*. Baltimore, Johns Hopkins Press.

— and Wingo, Lowdon, Jr. (eds.), 1968b. *Issues in Urban Economics*. Washington, D.C., Resources for the Future, Inc.

— (ed.), 1969. *The Quality of the Urban Environment*. Washington, D.C., Resources for the Future,Inc.

Pittsburgh Regional Planning Association, 1963a. *Economic Study of the Pittsburgh Region*. Pittsburgh, University of Pittsburgh Press.

—, 1963b. *Region in Transition*. Pittsburgh, University of Pittsburgh Press.

—, 1963c. *Region with a Future*. Pittsburgh, University of Pittsburgh Press.

Polikarpoff, G. G., 1966. *Radioactivity of Aquatic Organisms*. New York, Reinhold.

Robinson, E. A. G. (ed.), 1969. *Backward Areas in Advanced Countries*. London, Macmillan.

Roup, Phillip M., 1963. 'Satisfying the economic demands for natural resources: Some recent developments in European land policy.' In Ottoson, Howard W. (ed.), *Land Use Policy and Problems in the United States*. Lincoln, University of Nebraska Press.

Schlesinger, Arthur, Jr., 'Review of Carter Goodrich's Government promotion of American canals and railroads.' *Review of Economics and Statistics*, vol. 42, pp. 459-460.

SFI, 1969. 'Refuse disposal at sea?' *S.F.I. Bulletin*, no. 209. Washington, D.C., Sport Fishing Institute.

Sherman, Roger and Willet, Thomas D., 1968. *Regional Development, Externalities and Tax-Subsidy Combinations*. Harvard Institute of Economic Research, Discussion Paper, no. 35. Cambridge, Harvard University Press.

Stochfisch, J. A. and Edwards, D. J., 1969. 'The blending of public and private enterprise: The SST as a case in point.' *The Public Interest*, vol. 14, pp. 108-117.

Swenson, Robert W., 1968. 'The new conservation.' In Gates, Paul W. (ed.), *History*

of Public Law Development. Washington, D.C., U.S. Government Printing Office.
Tennessee Valley Authority (TVA), 1963. *An Appraisal of Coal Strip-Mining*. Knoxville, Tennessee Valley Authority.
—, 1969a. *Annual Report 1969*. Knoxville, Tennessee Valley Authority.
—, 1969b. *A Quality Environment in the Tennessee Valley*. Knoxville, Tennessee Valley Authority.
—, 1970. *Power Report*, Knoxville, Tennessee Valley Authority. See also: Clapp, 1955; Finer, 1964; Lilienthal, 1944; Moore, 1967; Wiersena, 1955.
Tiebout, Charles M., 1962. *The Community Economic Basic Study*. New York, Committee for Economic Development.
Turner, Frederick Jackson, 1894. 'The significance of the frontier in American history.' *Annual Report of the American Historical Association, 1893*. Washington, D.C., U.S. Government Printing Office.
United States (U.S.)
—, 1961. U.S. Congress. *Area Development Act*. Public Law 87-27. 87th Congress, First Session. Washington, D.C., U.S. Government Printing Office.
—, 1967. U.S. Department of Commerce, Economic Development Administration. *Report of the Independent Study Board on the Regional Effects of Government Procurement and Related Policies*. Washington, D.C., U.S. Government Printing Office.
—, 1968a. U.S. Department of Commerce and U.S. Department of Labor. 'Recent trends in social and economic conditions of negroes in the United States', *Current Population Reports*. Series P-23, no. 26; BLS Report no. 347. Washington, D. C., U.S. Government Printing Office.
—, 1968b. U.S. Department of the Interior, Fish and Wildlife Service. *Effects of Surface Mining on Fish and Wildlife in Appalachia*. Washington, D.C., U.S. Government Printing Office.
—, 1969a. U.S. Senate. *Regional Economic Development Legislation of 1969, Part I*. Hearings before the Subcommittee on Economic Development of the Committee on Public Works. Serial no. 91-5. Washington, D.C., U.S. Government Printing Office.
—, 1969b. U.S. Congress. *Highlights of the Public Works and Economic Development Act of 1965* (Public Law 89-136). 89th Congress, Fifth Session, Committee on Public Works, Committee Reprint no. 16. Washington, D.C., U.S. Government Printing Office.
U.S. News and World Report, 1969, June, pp. 96-99: 'A model city for Indian land'.
Upper Great Lakes Regional Commission (UGLRC). See: Berry, 1969.
White, Gilbert F., 1958. *Choice of Adjustment to Floods*. Department of Geography, Research Paper, no. 57. University of Chicago.
Widner, Ralph R. *et al.*, 1969. *Staff Evaluation Appalachian Regional Commission Program, 1965-1968*. Washington, D.C., Appalachian Regional Commission.
Wiersena, H., 1955. In Martin, G. C. (ed.), *TVA: The First Twenty Years*.
Winnick, Louis, 1966. 'Place prosperity vs. people prosperity: Welfare consideration in the geographic distribution of economic activity.' In: *Essays in Urban Land Economics*. In Honor of the 65th Birthday of Leo Grebler, Real Estate Research Program. Los Angeles, University of California.
Wollman, Nathaniel, 1962. *The Value of Water in Alternative Uses*. Albuquerque, University of New Mexico Press.
Young, Robert A., 1969. *Irrigation Needs and Federal Policies in the Arid West*. Discussion Paper. Washington, D.C., National Planning Commission.

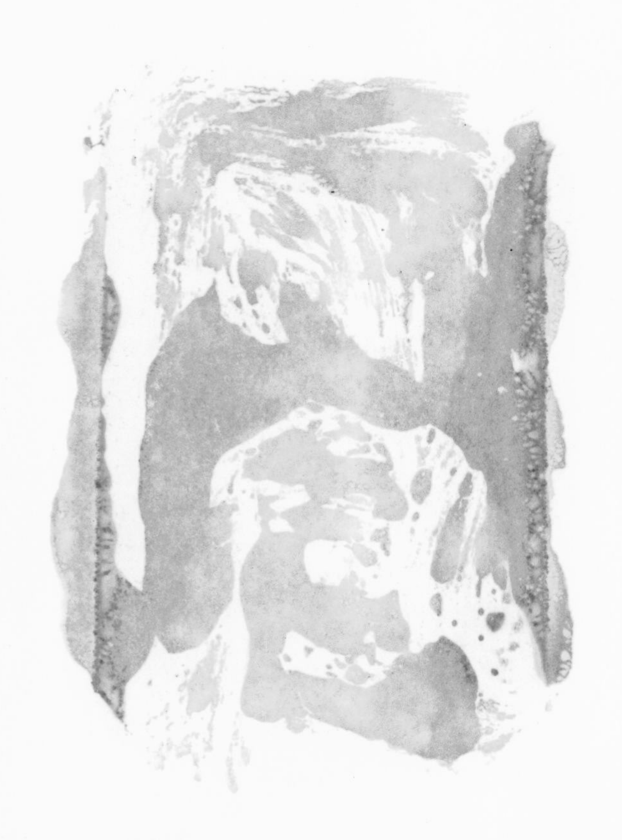